Wooden Floor Iıal

Everything you need to know about DIY wooden floors

Q&A's on Wooden Floors

PUBLISHED BY WOOD YOU LIKE LTD

Wooden Floor Installation Manual - Published by Wood You Like Ltd

Authors: Karin Hermans / Ton Slooven (Wood You Like Ltd)
Editor: Trevor Claringbold (Kudosmedia.org)
Digitising: Greenwood Graphics
Printed and bound: Lightning Source UK Ltd, Milton Keynes, United Kingdom
Floor type shown on front and back cover: Wood-Engineered Duoplank®
Oak Rustic A/B, bevelled, brushed & oiled Castle Grey

Copyright © 2010 Wood You Like Ltd
First edition printed 2010 in the United Kingdom

ISBN 978-0-9553473-4-4

No part of this book shall be reproduced or transmitted in any form or by any means, electronic or mechanical, including photocopying, recording, or by any information or retrieval system without written permission of the publisher.

Although every precaution has been taken in the preparation of this book, the publisher, authors and editor assume no responsibility for errors or omissions. Neither is any liability assumed for damages resulting from the use of the information contained herein.

Disclaimer: All advice given is for guidelines only. Wood You Like Ltd doesn't know the exact situation or circumstances of your home and/or quality of the products already there. Any person who relies upon any advice provided by Wood You Like Ltd given by email, or which is contained in any of Wood You Like's websites and publications does so entirely at their own risk. Wood You Like Ltd therefore accepts no duty or liability whatsoever, other than a duty to act honestly in good faith.

TESTIMONIALS

"Your advice was absolutely spot on, I did as you told me and not only have a laid the floor in the hall and passageway (it's a bungaloe), but did another two rooms after that, and the whole thing worked a treat! Best wishes"
Ross M.

"Thank you, you helped me loads... Have fit 2 rooms so far - just the kitchen to go! (another 30m2!!!!)"
James B.

"Unfortunately, I had already bought my wood when I found your guide.
However, your guide was probably the most helpful one I found for installation advice and other useful information, for which - thank you.
My job is now done, and I no longer need your advice. However, I shall be happy to point anyone interested in flooring towards your website and guide.
Mike S.

"Dear Karin, thank you very much for your help. Your business approach is a breath of fresh air and it is clearly only possible because you have a passion for your product and are interested in people rather than the isolated pursuit of profit! You therefore deserve to do well and, moreover, will have a more fulfilling business life as a result. Very impressed. Thank you"
Charlie

"Your advice was really, really useful in helping me to assess which fitter and supplier I would choose. I am just waiting for the quotations now."
Ansell L

"Your advice really helped us to make a decision about what type of wood flooring to choose. Especially as we have a number of issues with regard to the sub floor. Thanks!"
Adele B

"Thank you for your prompt reply and help. I wish you could also be in Spain!!"
Mielle E

"Thank you for your very generous advice - it's a great help as an inexperienced DIYer to know that there are people like Karin who can help answer my questions, from their knowledge and experience."
Sara H

"I was delighted with the help and advice that I received. It seemed to me that you cared that I should be successful in my efforts at wood floor installation. In addition, the information that I received in the guide confirmed much of what I believed but, more importantly, it shed light on aspects of installations that I was not familiar with."
Noel R

"Thanks to Wood You Like I scrutinised what I had bought; I only wish I'd listened to them sooner. It might have prevented me from buying my floor from a less than reputable company that went bankrupt a few days later......
Their advice for installation has confirmed what I had intended and given me the confidence I needed!"
Graham L

"I have now had my floor fitted and found your website and guide absolutely invaluable in deciding on what sort of floor, what sort of finish and how to fix it. Thank you."
Jacqui F

CONTENTS

INTRODUCTION
&
GENERAL ADVICE

INTRODUCTION & GENERAL ADVICE

Introduction to Guidebook

Welcome to Wood You Like's first Manual on natural wooden flooring, helping you choose who to select, and how to prepare, install and maintain it like a professional.

This comprehensive manual on installing natural wooden flooring contains all the tricks of the trade that we and other professionals use. It will help make your wood floor look like it was installed by a professional too.

It's based on our own experience of installing wooden floors for many years - both in our home country, The Netherlands, and now in the UK .

And who are we? Allow us to introduce the 'WWW' of Wood You Like Ltd: **W**ho we are, **W**here we come from, and **W**hy we do what we do the way we do it.

Who we are...
Wood You Like Ltd has two very 'hands-on' directors - both of Dutch origin:

Karin Hermans - *Managing Director* -
Karin will welcome you to the showroom, discuss the floor in question, and suggest which wood and finish types are suitable for your situation. Karin will always endeavour to answer any enquiries and questions you may have. She is also in charge of our marketing projects, from the informative website to writing specific wood flooring related articles, and is the author of the business novel "The Kiss Business - The Keep It Simple Sweetheart Principle in Business". (Available from Amazon.co.uk or direct from Wood You Like Ltd)

Ton Slooven - Director of Operations -
Ton is responsible for our quality control, planning the installation jobs, logistics, and is our most experienced professional installer. His speciality is Design Parquet.

Where we come from...
Both directors originate from the historic medieval town of Bergen op Zoom in the South-West of The Netherlands, close to the Belgium border. It's a picturesque town filled with many centuries-old buildings and treasures, and a wealth of traditions that have been handed down the generations.

Bergen op Zoom also has many long-established industries, including sugar refinery, cast iron work, farming and fishery. Most importantly, of course, it also produces excellent wooden flooring!

Bruynzeel flooring was founded in 1900, and added another parquet factory in the early 60's - Inpa Parket - which is still going strong. The Bruynzeel factory closed down in the late 70's, making many professionals redundant. A new type of industry was born - traditional wooden flooring retail shops, and professional independent installers. Both Ton and Karin have learned the ins and outs of the wooden flooring business from the most respected professionals there, including an apprenticeship in installing design parquet floors.

Beginning in 2000, they were employed by a new Dutch company that had plans to get a strong foothold in the domestic UK wood flooring market. However only two (rather large) retail showrooms were ever opened, and within 3 years the parent company decided to close both shops and focus their attention solely on the wholesale market.

After being made redundant, and strengthened by the ongoing support of their existing clients and business advisors, Ton and Karin decided to 'go-it-alone' and launched Wood You Like Ltd. Initially based from their home-office, in August 2005 they opened the showroom in the lovely village of Charing, near Ashford in Kent. Since then the company has continued to grow from strength to strength.

Why we do what we do the way we do it...
We are passionate about quality, and only source high quality products from equally 'passionate about quality' manufacturers. Manufacturers with their own FSC certified forests, with their own policies on reforestation, and their own quality control systems on producing the best products time after time after time. And we only work with 'passionate about quality' installers, too, and indeed with all the other essential team players.

In July 2008, FSC-UK.org issued Wood You Like Ltd an unique ID code: FSC-GBR-1019. This unique ID-code guarantees you that the products we label FSC certified are genuine, and it authorises Wood You Like to use the FSC-trademark. In order to receive this unique code, any retailer selling to domestic clients has to prove their purchases really do come directly from an FSC-certified company or manufacturer. (FSC: The wood in this product comes from well managed forests independently certified in accordance with the rules of the Forest Stewardship Council.)

Time after time you will find special products and services in our company. Special in the way the product is constructed, or proven by its quality and method. We will discuss these construction and installation methods later in this manual. Even standard products, like solid floorboards, are treated as special. We know why a 180mm wide board that is only 15mm thick will cause problems, and we know how wide is wide enough to prevent problems.

We are members of the BwfA - British wood flooring Association:

The British Wood Flooring Association represents the interest of professionals specialising in the wood flooring sector. Installers and suppliers of wood flooring have united within BwfA to ensure that quality standards in this growing sector meet the expectations of consumers.

The aims of the association are:

- The establishment of an industry code of practice to be adopted by all BwfA members.
- Recognised training and accreditation standards.
- Assistance and support for installers in their business.
- Continuous and influential dialogue with the wood flooring market.
- International representation for the industry and involvement in development of standards.
- Promotion of the benefits of real wood flooring to the consumer.

So that's us, and our three W's: **W**ho, **W**here and **W**hy. Our passion about quality, and our dedication to informing our (DIY) clients on every aspect of natural wooden flooring is second nature to us. Nowhere is this better demonstrated than on our informative website, FAQ & news blog, and through our many articles both on and off line.

This manual is, in fact, based on a compilation of our answers to questions that we've often been asked by DIY-ers (and even other floor installers) from all over the UK. We have - where needed - added more tips, rules of thumb and advice on the various subjects. During a recent survey of our many contacts, we asked "Do you know of any disaster stories?"

The responses highlighted the most common reason for a disaster was not making the correct preparations at the right time. This was closely followed by not reading the instructions on the tin, bottle, pack or any other such packaging materials provided by the manufacturer or supplier. And all of these disasters are problems that could have been very easily prevented, saving everyone time, money, and a lot of hassle!

Installing a wood floor yourself isn't rocket-science. However, it is a known fact that the better quality you buy, the quicker and easier the installation is. To our way of thinking, that's kind of obvious!

So, to put it another way - the choice is yours:

- Go for a lesser quality, and struggle - or have a professional install your floor, which could still turn it into a reasonable result.
- Or buy better quality and install the floor like a professional yourself, and the quality of the product will be your highly valued assistant!

This manual contains advice on preparation, installation and maintenance, plus information about the various floor types, different choices of underfloor, and much, much more.

- Learn how to tackle underfloor problems.
- Know what to look for when purchasing your materials.
- Use the check-lists before you start with the job:
- The correct preparations.
- The correct tools and materials.
- The correct schedule of works.
- Discover the 'tricks of the trade' that will make seemingly difficult obstacles easy to execute.
- Finish your floor to the highest quality.
- And all in plain English, with clear images where needed to explain even more.

You are more than welcome to ask us something by using our special question form, which can be found on our website ("ask for personal advice"), or by simply sending us an email.

For Design Parquet flooring (installation) we would like to point you towards our existing wood-guides online. We do cover repair and restoration subjects in this guidebook.

Kind Regards

Wood You Like Ltd
Karin Hermans / Ton Slooven
www.wood-you-like.co.uk

How this Manual came about, Extra Bonus and Where to find What

Being involved on a daily basis with all aspects of natural wooden flooring, and noticing the growing influence of online information (some correct and some incorrect - neither Google nor your web browser knows the difference), we started to answer questions about wooden flooring on various DIY forums (especially Ebuild: www.ebuild.co.uk, and DIY-not: www.diynot.com) at the end of 2004. Questions ranged from confusion about products, confusion about contradicting advice from suppliers, instructions on the materials, to cries for help after an installation had gone horribly wrong.

How Information can turn into Knowledge

This lack of proper and honest information made us realise even more how important knowledge is, and by using the (then) latest web technology we launched our own blog about natural wooden flooring which we called the FAQ & News site: Everything you always wanted to know about wooden flooring but didn't know where or whom to ask. (http://faq.woodyoulike.co.uk)

As we mentioned in the Introduction, our survey "Do you know any disaster stories?" highlighted the most common reason for a disaster was not making the correct preparations at the right time, and all of these disasters are problems that could have been very easily prevented, saving everyone time, money, and a lot of hassle!

Now you can search and find plenty of information online, but that does not always mean you can or will learn how to tackle or prevent problems. This is especially true if your type of problem or situation is anything but "standard". As suppliers and installers, we know that every home and even every design wish can be unique, and it deserves an unique solution - not a "one-fits-all" answer or product.

For that reason we launched our blog first, where we invited readers to submit their questions into the "comment-box". These questions we answered personally, making sure we focused only on the "situation at hand".

A short while later we created a special page on our main website for the same reason - to invite readers to receive personal advice from us. The queries came flooding in! From asking for advice on which wood species or floor type would best suit a certain home, to whole stories filled with such misery that it almost broke our heart (we're very sensitive people!). There is so much information out there on the wibbly wobbly web, and yet still so little real knowledge. The sudden rise in wood flooring "supermarkets" jumping on the band wagon didn't help either. Pile them high; sell them low; and who cares if the punter ends up with rubbish?

After answering question after question for three years we decided to create a simple but comprehensive installation guide, and to make this not only available to our own DIY-clients, but to anyone planning to install a wooden floor in the best possible way. This guide (in a simple PDF format, delivered by email) was launched in December 2008, and was an instant success.

It also triggered more questions. So we kept adding to the guide, which became more and more a collection of questions and answers grouped in a few logical categories. Late in 2009 we decided it was time to completely overhaul the guide, and make it available not only as a PDF, but also as a proper paperback. So now you can have it handy by your side while you're working on your floor. The end result is what you have in your hands right now.

Of course words can only describe so much, and images can sometimes tell a much better, more complete story. But filling this book with images would have increased its price tremendously, so - also knowing how many DIY-ers have internet access - we came up with a much simpler solution:

Extra "Bonus" Materials Online

Buying this paperback entitles you to an extra bonus: Online access to colour images, interior design pictures, work in progress photos, detailed drawings, and much more. All you have to do to get access to this extra information is to go to our special website: www.woodmanual.co.uk, click on the link 'Extras', submit your name and email address, and an email containing the log-in details will magically whiz its way to your inbox.

In all the chapters which have extra information online, we've added this little note: 'Extra info available online'. If you read this, you know you only have to log-in, find the relevant article (with the same title as in the book) and if needed or required download the PDF that comes with it.

What could be simpler?

Where to Find What in the Manual

Besides the normal index telling you on which page you can find which chapter or article we though a short overview of subjects and keywords might come in handy. So:

Introduction & General Advice
That's the section you're reading now (good, isn't it?!) It contains a list of all the benefits wooden flooring gives you - in case you weren't convinced yet. This is followed by more general tips and advice on life and design style, and which wood floor, and wood type, would suit your style best. In this "general" section we also dive into the differences

between floor types, such as solid versus wood-engineered, what effect different grades in wood have on price (and stability), plus an explanation and history on oil versus varnish.

The section ends with tips for before you begin the actual works, and how to calculate how much material you need.

Preparations

A very important section! Although most items in here seem tedious - because they end up invisible under your new wood floor - it is absolutely imperative you read through this. It may be only to discover that, in your case, most preparations are not needed (wouldn't that be a nice surprise?), but don't take chances... read it!

It offers plenty of advice about the underfloor, how to prepare the best base for the best end result, the best schedule to plan all the works involved, and what to note when you purchase (or plan to purchase) solid floorboards.

Installation of Floorboards: the Basics

Now here's where the fun starts. Tips and advice on the actual job of installing your wood floor in the best way possible. We dive into expansion gaps, (not literally, you understand!), and the various installation methods and other "decide before you do" matters.

Using the "Floating" Method.

The method most DIY-ers will use, and one that involves the least extra materials. There's a special article on how to glue the T&G correctly - read this before you even open a bottle of PVAC wood glue. Then, keep it simple, follow common sense, and take your time installing board by board, row by row. This section is filled with tricks of the trade, from installing that last row to why to take a tea/coffee break - and when.

Using the "Glue Down" Method

A different method for different circumstances. This section focuses on the correct extra materials and tools, and how to use them. This method is often used when there is Underfloor Heating involved, so it includes a fact sheet on how to treat your UFH system before, during, and after the installation of your wood floor - plus a case-study by one of our clients. Learn from their hands on experience and get the same good results that they established.

Using the "Secret Nail" Method

Again, a different method for different circumstances. Installing directly onto joists? Then these are the chapters for you! This section starts off with a myth, and explains why a decent concrete floor does not need battens in order to install a wood floor.

Finishing Unfinished Floors

All about sanding, which finishing product to use when (HardWaxOil or a single oil), and advice on the best - in our opinion the only - sanding equipment to use. Hire-centers be warned!

Maintenance

Every wood floor needs maintenance, but only once every 5 - 6 months. That means every wood floor, including those with a varnished/lacquered finish. Don't be told otherwise! Fortunately, maintenance is so simple and so rewarding. Your grateful floor will become more beautiful with every little bit of TLC you bestow on it. This section contains - of course - our tips and advice on preventive, regular and major maintenance (major only for those cases where you neglected the regular maintenance for a long while).

Trouble shooting

Yes, indeed. No manual can ever cover every single unique situation that you might encounter, but rest assured we've covered the most FAQ and circumstances as described by our website and blog readers. This section has a collection of specific Q&A's we found worthwhile to add without the need of extensive details or separate articles. And if you find something essential is missing for your own unique situation, just give us a shout through the special "Ask Personal Advice" page on our website - and we'll help out to the best of our knowledge.

Resources:

Things not to expect from your wood floor - only 4 things, but important nonetheless to prevent disappointment. In this section you will also find contact details and references to our websites.

Extras:

Discovered an original parquet floor in your home? Then this section is for you. Two guides for existing parquet floors, one on cleaning and maintaining this valuable floor covering, and one if your floor is in need of some repairs.

Have fun and remember to claim your access to all the extra information online: www.woodmanuals.co.uk (and click on 'extras').

Benefits of Wooden Flooring in 6 Facts

[Extra info available online - www.woodmanual.co.uk]

This is the only robust floor covering that becomes more beautiful over time!

Adding new or restored natural wooden flooring will definitely increase the value and comfort of any house or home immediately... yes, even yours!

It's a known fact - even before the 'credit-crunch' effect was felt on the housing market.

Fact 1:

Abbey National (now part of Santander) recently asked 100 Estate Agents "Which home improvements do they consider add most value to a home?"

The results were somewhat surprising, showing that it's not the large projects like extensions or expensive kitchens that add the most value. In fact, in their opinion these often tend to lose money - as much as 50% of their cost! No, what does increase value has more to do with adding 'lifestyle' features, as it's those that provide the greatest return when it comes to valuing or selling a house.

The survey showed that "For every £1,000 spent on 'lifestyle' features, you can reckon on adding more than £3,500 to the value of your home."

Why? Well, because most people envy, and would like to buy into, those signals of 'success' so effortlessly portrayed by lifestyle 'visuals'. Features such as wooden flooring - which is light and hygienic, provides a sense of space and elegance, is wonderfully easy to keep clean and dust free, and is exceptionally robust and long lasting – can make a huge difference to the value of your home.

And talking of wooden flooring, according to a recent study done by WoodCare, adding wooden features to your home will increase its value 5% - 15%, almost immediately.

> "You achieve an instant positive effect by stripping down and exposing the natural character of wooden banisters, re-instating those genuine wooden doors, and, particularly, installing real wooden floors (especially in the reception areas)". They said.

It's not just that you can get a better price for your house than your neighbour (unless he also has a nice wood floor!). Estate agents and existing clients tell us again and again that homes with wooden floors **sell quicker!** If you'll allow us to throw another survey result at you, "Ninety percent of estate agents said that houses with wooden flooring are more marketable, 58% agreed that homes with wooden floors sell for more money, and 46% agreed that homes with wooden floors sell more quickly than those without."

Potential buyers know the benefits of wooden flooring as well as you do, so when offered the choice between a house that already has (professionally) installed real wooden floors, and a similar house without wooden flooring (and which will then cost them more money, effort and time to add themselves), which one do you think will sell quicker and for more? If you've been paying attention, it's an obvious answer of course.

Even if the colour of the wood floor isn't exactly to their liking, your buyer will know (and if he doesn't, of course you'll tell him!) that it's easier and cheaper to change it - with coloured polish to start with, and perhaps followed later by sanding the floor and applying another colour - than to have to rip out carpet, buy and install a wooden floor and delay the moving date.

It's a 'buyers-market' nowadays - profit from it and offer your buyer the obvious choice, selling it for your price and quickly.

Rental-property owners: Your potential tenant will perceive your property as more luxurious when you have real wooden flooring installed, and hence should be willing to pay more rent for it - increasing your ROI instantly.

Fact 2:

Real wooden flooring is one of the **most anti-allergic floor coverings** there is. Over the last decennia there has been an increase in the numbers of people suffering from allergies, eczema and asthma.

House dust is the major cause of allergy in people with year-long runny or blocked noses, and/or sneezing. In addition to these allergic reactions, dust can trigger and irritate asthma and eczema. A speck of dust may contain fabric fibres, human skin, bacteria, animal danders, pollen, grains, moulds spores, food particles, mites and mite-droppings. Mites cannot be seen without a microscope. They thrive in warm and humid conditions. Because they feed on skin scales, they love bedding, carpets, upholstered furniture, clothing, closets and car seats. They usually survive ordinary vacuuming because they burrow deep and are equipped with sucking pads on their feet.

In 2006, the Dispatches programme on Channel 4 dedicated a two-part program to the increasing problem of **"How to beat your kids Asthma"**. All specialists who were consulted strongly advised to rip out carpets and vinyl - a major source of toxic and sometimes persistent substances in the environment, known to trigger attacks - and to replace it with wooden floors immediately.

Offering yourself, your children, and your potential buyers a floor covering that doesn't trigger any attacks, and one that is known to reduce the suffering of allergies and eczema almost immediately, is the most practical and health-improving decision you can take.

No more constant sneezing, no more wheezing, and no more itchy skin are the most simple effects. That's without more serious risks - such as how life-threatening a severe asthma attack can be.

Rental-property owners: The same goes for you. How many potential tenants might suffer from allergies, eczema or asthma? By offering them your property with the most anti-allergic floor covering around you improve the chance of renting it out **tenfold.**

Fact 3:

No floor covering is **easier to clean** than natural wooden flooring. Long gone are the days of polishing a wood floor on hands and knees, or seeing 'skid-marks'. The modern finishing and maintenance materials have taken care of that.

A soft broom is all it takes for normal day to day care - easier done than dragging your vacuum cleaner out of the cupboard (sometimes smelling of dust). And - **clean is clean** - no hidden dust or dirt like you can have with carpets.

It's also an ideal floor covering when you have pets, as one of our clients discovered:

"I still don't know how I coped before, during the moulting periods of my cats and dogs, when we had carpets! Since we have wooden floors it takes **no effort at all**, just one simple sweep of a broom."

Spillages and little accidents are wiped off, cleaned away in no time at all without having to turn to chemicals. Calling for a carpet-cleaning company is a thing of the past, as is getting so frustrated with a persistent stain that the only option seems to replace the carpet or place an extra rug on top of it. (And knowing Murphy's Law - those accidents always tend to happen just before you're about to entertain the largest crowd ever in your home.)

Regular maintenance (roughly once every 5 to 6 months) will keep your floor healthy, and even better protected against dirt and drips.

There is another well known fact too. Every bit of TLC you spend on your natural wooden floor will increase its beauty, its lustre, and its durability. It's as simple as that. Compare that with a carpet of just one or two years old, and you'll see the extra advantage wooden flooring gives you immediately.

Rental-property owners: Some tenants are just not careful enough with property belonging to someone else - sad, but true, as many of you will be well aware of. Another known fact is that dirty surfaces attract more dirt. In other words, once a carpet looks worn, slightly damaged and dirty, nobody is really going to care if it gets even dirtier or more damaged.

But, a floor covering that always looks clean, and off of which spillages are easily removed, tends to bring out the feeling of 'ownership'. Your tenants will take better care of 'their' lovely wooden floor than they will with a carpet. So no more need to replace the carpets every year, saving you rather a lot of money, grievance and aggravation in one simple go.

Fact 4:

Wooden floors are also called the best **'solid investment'** you can add to your house, lasting you 30 - 40 years! If that's not a first class **R**eturn **O**n **I**nvestment, we don't know what other floor covering is.

Natural wooden flooring, taken care of properly (and that's another benefit - it's easy to care for) is the most **durable** floor covering you can have, increasing in beauty over the years.

Fact 5:

Natural wooden floors are NOT slippery (despite many people assuming they are), but come with the extra advantage of having a smooth surface on which furniture can be easily moved around. Adding protective felt-guards to legs of the chairs or tables doesn't make them slip away underneath you, but simply eases the effort needed when moving them.

Many elderly and physically impaired clients have remarked on this pleasing fact. Since installing wooden floors, heavy chairs - or even normal dining chairs - are no longer an obstacle for them. They just 'ease' away when you need to move them for vacuum cleaning, for example, and are no longer awkward when sitting down for breakfast, lunch or dinner.

Rental-property owners: The 'grey-generation' will live independently longer and longer. When 'down-grading' in property (because their own house is becoming too large to handle easily), an increasing number will be looking for luxurious, comfortable living accommodation.

Making their daily living circumstances easier by installing wooden floors to your property adds to their comfort, allowing them to stay independent for even more years, and hence renting your property for a longer term.

Fact 6:

Most natural wooden floorings are eco-friendly. All Wood You Like's wooden flooring, from **Basic Oak to Bespoke**, comes from sustainable sources, be it FSC or PEFC certified. Thanks to sustainable forest management, more trees are planted than are harvested. In fact, European re-forestation grows by an area the size of Cyprus every year!

Remember - Adding natural wooden flooring increases the value of your house, and the comfort of your home immediately.
It's the most eco-friendly, easy to clean, anti-allergic, durable floor covering around. A beautiful 'Solid Investment' on all aspects, with an above average Return On Investment - giving you years and years of comfortable living.

A Wood Floor for Every Design and Lifestyle

[Extra info available online - www.woodmanual.co.uk]

Question:

I would love a really good wood floor. I have two dogs and am looking to do the living room. I would like the wood to be finished, what would you recommend as the best product for my needs.

Answer:

Wooden flooring is definitely the best option when you have pets like dogs and cats. Many of our clients remark on the ease of removing the hairs etc from the floor covering when their pets are moulting.

I would suggest an oil finish, wet paw marks won't show immediately - which they do on lacquered floors - and when maintenance is applied regularly your floor becomes even more beautiful.

Our most popular floor is a Wood-Engineered Oak Rustic wide-board, brushed and oiled naturally - full of character, easy to clean and suitable for almost every area.

A Man's Home is his Castle

Today's world can be very hectic and demanding: work, children, school-runs, holidays, TV-programs that everyone tells you you must see, books to read, social contacts to keep up... and that's just before lunch! No wonder your home is still regarded as your castle. A place to retreat to, or to entertain in.

If you like entertaining, having guests for dinner, or throwing a lively party, you don't want to worry about spillages. At the same time you want your home to be a very welcoming, even cosy place. Natural Wooden Flooring will give any home a warm, rich and friendly feeling, and due to its easy maintenance the worry about spillages is one less thing to concern you.

For many people, especially with small children, practicality is the key issue when choosing a floor covering. But wood combines practicality with functionality.

For family rooms where children can play, do their homework, or watch TV, Natural Wooden Flooring is an ideal choice. Wood is a living product and will adapt its temperature to its surroundings. It's never too cold, or too warm. Lots of (small) colourful rugs can make it really special, and if you select rugs with a children's theme, like princesses or pirates, it will become part of their adventures.

A warmer colour wood (smoked, warm gold-brown) will make this room very inviting. And yet very easy to keep clean and dust free, ideal for the increasing numbers of asthmatic or allergic children. (Remember, that may not be your children - but could well be their friends who come to play).

Some types of floors need more attention than others. If you're a bizy-bizy person in a busy household, you don't want to be spending much time on keeping your floor looking spotless. Very light coloured floors (Maple, Ash) show stains and marks very easily, while very dark floors show up the dust. Floors with a lacquer finish will also show (especially wet) marks sooner than floors with an oil/wax finish.

Suits your Style - Any Style you Might Have.

No matter what style you have (or are going to have) there will be a perfect Natural Wooden Floor to compliment it.

Minimalism design just asks for a prime grade with unobtrusive, simple grain. Small boards without bevelled edges will create a smooth harmonious surface, without looking unnatural.

Country kitchens will benefit from rich warm colours, from honey Oak with lots of knots, to the wide variation in colour of a Rustic Iroco/Kambala floor.

Chic apartments with modern clean furniture will go perfectly with a light coloured wood - European or Canadian Maple, warm pinkish Steamed Beech or the pale Ash.

But nothing can beat the good-old Oak floor. It suits any design style, be it minimalism, contemporary, country, Art-Deco or Georgian and Edwardian. Oak has a rich choice in grades where, for instance, the prime grade will compliment contemporary and minimalism, and where the extra rustic will enhance your County-style design.

Whatever your style, keep an eye on the era of your property. Make sure your decoration matches it, especially when you're thinking of moving up on the property ladder.

Natural Wooden Flooring creates a clean, uncluttered feel. It can transform a living space, bringing calm and order where chaos once reigned! Choose a wooden floor that works well with your existing interior design, and vary the species or the colouring to suit a room's function. Feel free to browse in our showroom, to help select the wood and colour best suited for your style.

From Solid to Veneer

Question:
Still undecided about installing a wooden engineered floor in my hall. My biggest concern is people coming in and out wearing high heels. I figured that laminate would be a better option. I would welcome your advice.

Answer:
The main problem is not the type of floor, the problem is damaged high heels. Normal high heels hardly have an effect, but the moment the protection of the pin is damaged it can cause indentations in the floor.

In regards of what can withstand this type of damage better, and what can be resolved or repaired easiest: wood-engineered, definitely.

The problem with laminate flooring is once the thin top layer is damaged, your whole floor is, in most cases, damaged beyond repair. With a wood-engineered floor, especially one with an oiled finish, any small damage can be repaired locally, and indentations will not result in a floor that has lost its protective layer (when regular maintenance is applied).

What's in a Name?

We know from experience that there is sometimes confusion over the terminology that certain suppliers/retailers and (DIY)forum members use to describe a floor type.

The main confusion is about laminated flooring - a term used by DIY-ers (and even some suppliers) for both **Melamine Laminated** Flooring (the 'plastic' Melamine stuff with only a photo-copy of wood on the surface), and for Wood-Engineered and Wood-Veneered flooring (flooring with a solid wood top layer between 0.2mm and 6 – 8mm with a crossed-backing of pine/plywood or hdf).

In the (English) wood-flooring profession, 'laminate' is used to describe the Melamine flooring (like Pergo, Quick-step etc).

The term **Wood-Veneer** is used when the solid wooden top layer has a thickness between 0.2 to 2mm.

Wood-Engineered covers the rest of the 'engineered' flooring, where the solid wooden top layer is more than 2mm thick (and can go up to even 8mm), but has a crossed-backing of a different material to that of the top layer.

Real wood is sometimes used to describe Wood-Engineered and Wood-Veneer flooring, as opposed to the Melamine Laminated flooring.

Misuse of term 'Parquet'. Where in the mainland of Europe 'Parquet' (Parket) means wooden flooring (any wooden flooring, from solid, wood-engineered to wood block design patterns like herringbone), in the UK the term Parquet is commonly used to describe the latter - i.e. wood blocks in any design pattern.

We've noticed, however, that some manufacturers and retailers use the term Parquet in the UK to promote the 3-strip Wood-Engineered (or 3-strip Wood-Veneer) flooring. This can lead to disappointed customers, who were expecting a real (solid) 'old-fashioned' parquet floor instead of the tongue and groove (or click) boards they are in fact purchasing.

Solid Tongue & Groove Floorboards

These boards are made out of the **same material** (Oak, Maple etc), with Tongues or Grooves on all four sides (although some manufacturers/saw-mills still create them only on the two long sides).

Several wooden strips glued together (2- or 3-strip), or a plank composed out of two or three layers of the same material, are also part of this group, and are usually called **'composed floorboards'**.

Solid boards come either unfinished, where you can choose your own kind of finish (i.e. lacquer, varnish, HardWaxOil or several layers of hard wax), or pre-finished. Some unfinished floors need sanding with 100 or even 80 grit abrasives before the finish can be applied. Wood You Like's unfinished floors normally come filled and sanded. Most solid boards have bevelled edges on the long sides, some even on all four sides.

The maximum width of a solid board is 10 times the thickness of the board (i.e. 20mm thick is maximum 200mm wide). Any wider and there is a higher risk of cupping.

A solid board can be installed:

- **Floating (glueing the T&G)** if the area is not wider than 5 - 6 meters, and preferably done by a professional floor fitter who knows what he/she is doing.

- **Glued down** using flexible adhesive and a correctly notched trowel - as long as your concrete/screed floor is sound and level (the weakest link is the quality of the concrete/screed!).

- **Nailed down** directly onto joists (if the thickness of the board is 18mm or thicker, and the joists are not further apart than 35 - 40 cm centre to centre). If using this latter method make sure you are supplied with long enough planks, because one plank must connect with a minimum of three joists.

Solid boards can be installed in all rooms and areas where there is **no risk of excessive moisture** (so NOT bathrooms, en-suites, utility-rooms or kitchens), or rapid changes in temperature (conservatories, hallways).

Wood You Like doesn't recommend Solid floorboards to be installed over underfloor heating.

Wood-Engineered Boards

This type of floor has a Solid Wood top layer with a (crossed) backing of one or two other types of material, like pine, MDF, HDF, OSB, cork or plywood. Some manufactures have started to introduce the click-system, but most still come with Tongue and Groove on all four sides.

The thickness of the Solid top layer ranges from 0.6mm (what Wood You Like calls **'veneer'**) to 3.6mm (standard on most products), and even to 6mm (like the Duoplank boards).

The 'standard' 'Wood-Engineered' board is 2- or 3-strip, but more and more manufacturers have introduced the full plank with bevelled edges that, once installed, has the same appearance as a solid plank.

Most Wood-Engineered floors come pre-finished, lacquered or varnished, but the demand in the U.K. for oil-finish is on the increase. Some manufacturers even supply unfinished Wood-Engineered full planks.

Wood-Engineered floors can be installed:

- **Floating (glueing the T&G)** if the area is not wider than 10 - 11 meters.

- **Glued down** using flexible adhesive and a correctly notched trowel - as long as your concrete/screed floor is sound and level (the weakest link is the quality of the concrete/screed!).

- **Nailed down** directly on joists (if the thickness of the board is 18mm or thicker, and the joists are not further apart than 35 - 40 cm centre to centre). If using this latter method make sure you are supplied with long enough boards, because one board must connect with a minimum of three joists.

Wood-Engineered floors can be installed **in all rooms and areas**, most of them also in kitchens, utility-rooms and conservatories because of the increased stability of the (crossed) backing. Wood You Like doesn't recommend Wood Engineered with MDF backing to be used in bathrooms or en-suites.

Most of the Wood-Engineered floors are suitable for installing on underfloor heating. The Duoplank Oak range is guaranteed on underfloor heating.

Parquet Flooring

Originally this name is given to unfinished **solid planks/strips/tiles without Tongue & Groove**, which are either glued and nailed on a plywood or special chipboard sub floor, or glued directly onto a concrete/screed underfloor (like mosaic tiles, herringbone or other patterns). The planks/strips/tiles are 6 to 10mm thick, and are known in The Netherlands and Belgium as Overlay floors.

After installing, the floor is sanded three (or more) times. First with an abrasive grit 40, then with a grit 80 (and the sand-dust collected). Between the second and the third sanding the collected sand-dust is mixed with a special wood-filler and 'plastered' onto the floor to fill every gap and nail hole. After the third sanding (with a grit 100 or 120), the oil-finish is applied. If you plan to apply a lacquer/varnish finish, then sand a 4th time with grit 150.

It is possible to use bevelled planks, but then the filling of the nail holes has to be done plank-by-plank - or even hole by hole.
Usually the pattern/tile floors come with borders in a different pattern, and a small strip of a different wood (like very dark Wenge) to accentuate the floor.

Grades, Ways of Sawing, Areas and their Influence on Wood Floors - and Your Choice

[Extra info available online - www.woodmanuals.co.uk]

Question:
I have just bought some engineered oak flooring 189mm x 22mm prefinished, the sample I got looked fine, when I collected the order it was all shrink wrapped and no finished surface was visible.
When I unwrapped it I was dismayed to say the least, now I used to work with oak many years ago and know it has "features" but I think this is awful, there are knots (or have been) that have been filled, many are up to 50mm diameter and are just a puddle of dark brown filler no sign of the original knot/timber remains, some of the planks are golden some are brown, one even has a full size imprint of a boot tread sealed in, there are some shakes up to 10mm wide running 2/3rds the length of the plank (1.8m). this was not described as rustic or distressed by the way, do you think I can reject this as unfit for purpose?

Answer:
The description you give of the received floor sounds like what we call County Grade, or Extra Rustic: knots can be up to 60mm, many colour variations but NO fabrication damages. Normal Rustic may have knots as large as 30mm and colour variations, but again NO fabrication damages

If I were you I would return the stuff a.s.a.p, together with a covering note indicating 'Returned as Quality received not per sample'.

Wood comes in many species, and wooden floors are available in many types and colours. Some characteristics of how wood is made, or engineered, into a wood floor can determine the price, stability, and even in which areas you can or cannot install a specific floor.

This chapter will highlight three important characteristics of wooden floors - grades, the way a board is sawn from the tree, and the resilience of floor types in specific areas of your home. All, of course, major considerations when you are selecting your wooden floor.

How a Tree is Sawn into Planks Affects Price and Stability

A tree can be divided in three specific areas: bark, annual rings, heart or centre

And into two major ways of cutting:

1) Across the grain in blocks which will show the annual rings of the tree as if you are looking down onto the trunk. It is not the most cost effective way of cutting a tree, and therefore the price of so-called "end-grain" floors is rather higher than radial sawn wood.

In earlier days the end-grain of logs were used as "chopping blocks" (because the tough end-grain surface could withstand the pounding of hammers without splintering), and even as street-paving! Later they were frequently used as industrial floor covering because of their durability, and for many industries it was a worthwhile investment until more modern (and cheaper) hard wearing solutions became available.

2) With the grain in boards or planks, either radial or tangential, which can again be divided in three ways:

Quarter Sawn

The log is cut at right angles (as far as is possible) to the heart. Sap canals (medullary rays) show as 'mirrors' or 'flecks'. There is a lot of saw-waste in this cutting-process, which translates in the price, but the planks are very stable.

The medullary rays are very specific to Oak, and it's one way to distinguish Oak from Chestnut - also called **"Poor men's Oak"** because of the stark resemblance to Oak. Chestnut is however softer than Oak, and doesn't have any medullary rays in boards cut radially.

Note: when applying a colour finish to an Oak floor that contains many "mirrors", your result could make this characteristic more pronounced. This is because the grain structure of the mirror is different than the surrounding wood. Depending on the colour, the mirrors could show either darker or lighter, so be aware of this.

Half-Quarter Sawn

The log is cut headlong, and afterwards cut into planks. One side of the plank shows one half of the grain. It's lower in price than quarter sawn, and has medium stability.

Tangential (dosse)

The log is simply cut in planks, like most pine boards are. It has a very pronounced grain, and this type of cutting can react more to changes in humidity than the two above. Is lower in price, but also in stability.

Note: These are frequently used in 'cheap offers' of solid or wood-engineered Oak floors. The finished result is rather dull in character because there is hardly any variation in the boards. Oak floors from our suppliers always contain a mix of all cutting ways to give your floor the true, authentic, and characteristic appearance you expect of it.

Ways of Sawing, and their Appearance in Grades

Depending on your personal preferences in style, the following standard grading characteristics (especially of Oak flooring) can help you select the most suited grade for your home.

Excellence, Elegant, Diamond, Harvest, Cottage, Exquisite or even Cambridge, or Copenhagen. Grade names to inform you about the characteristics of the wooden floor you are choosing? Or perhaps why one so-called grade costs more than the other? We don't use fantasy or grand names. We use, as much as possible, the classification in grades most of the manufacturers use and which tell you what characteristics you can expect in the floor you buy.

Prime (or Select)
Hardly any colour differences, no knots or sapwood (means lighter, sometimes even white colour along the grain). The floor contains mostly quarter sawn and half-quarter sawn boards, with some dosse sawn boards. This grade is frequently used for herringbone and other patterns that uses small blocks. If only quarter and half-quarter wood is used, the grade of the floor is sometimes called "Exquisite", so that it stands out more from the normal Prime grade.

Nature
Some colour differences, some closed knots not larger than 15mm, and sapwood is allowed. The floor contains a mix of different sawn boards.

Rustic
Colour differences, closed and open knots up to 60mm, some sapwood and tiny dry-cracks are allowed. The floor contains mostly half-quarter and dosse sawn boards, with some quarter sawn board possible.

Industrial
Colour differences, large open and closed knots, sapwood, beetle holes, manufacturing mistakes or damage, and size differences (width) allowed. The floor contains all sawn methods with these characteristics in the boards. It's frequently used for mosaic tiles when used as subfloor for herringbone or other pattern floors. Some suppliers/manufacturers sell this grade as the so-called 'Wagon-boards'.

Rustic and Rustic, not always the same

The grade in Oak which gives the most confusion (and arguments between honest retailers and others) is when Rustic isn't really Rustic any more, but more of an industrial grade. A truly rustic Oak floor should not contain large open knots, and no machine damages should be present. We have seen descriptions under the term Rustic that we would definitely class as Industrial.

The price-tag of "rustic" floors can give you a first impression of the real grade you can expect when purchasing such a floor. If it sounds too good to be true (i.e. cheap), then generally that's exactly what it is... not true.

Requesting a sample of the product on offer does not always help either. Samples can only show so much of what your whole floor will look like in the end. Be aware that it is very easy for suppliers to be 'selective' when offering samples!

The EU is trying hard to get some regulated standardising in the use of grade names, with minimum and maximum size of knots, amount of sapwood, etc.

Prior to this regulation, many European manufacturers have already agreed on differentiation between Rustic and Rustic:

Rustic A/B – closed knots up to 30mm.
Rustic C/D – closed and open knots up to 60mm.

But no machine damage in any of the true rustic grades. C/D grade is also frequently called 'Extra rustic', or any other - sometimes fancy - name, like 'County'.

Tropical Wood Species

Tropical Wood normally comes in two grades: Prime or Rustic.

Prime here means hardly any colour differences between the floorboards, where as Rustic in Tropical wood means that (many) colour differences between boards are allowed (like the yellow streaks in Rustic Merbau). Only some of the tropical woods have knots, and if any are found in the boards it's normally in the Rustic grade.

Areas and their Influence on Your Choice in Wooden Flooring

Natural Wooden Flooring is a suitable, hygienic floor covering for most areas in the home or commercial premises (like offices, reception areas, retail showrooms, etc.). Wood You Like doesn't recommend the use of it in so-called 'wet-rooms' but when proper care is taken wooden floors can be installed in larger family bathrooms and/or cloakrooms.

Sometimes a Specific Area means a Restriction of Choice

Solid wood floors are suitable for most areas, **except** where rapid changes in temperature (hallways, conservatories) happen, or where the normal air-humidity tends to be higher than in other rooms (kitchens, utility rooms, bathrooms, cloakrooms).

In those areas, *wood-engineered* floors or *original parquet* floors are preferred due to the stability the construction of these products gives compared to solid floorboards. Although original parquet floors are, in fact, solid wooden floors, the original method of glueing (and most times also nailing) the woodblocks of 6mm to 10mm thick on 8mm solid wood mosaic tiles (or small chipboard-plywood sheets in some circumstances) creates a cross-backed subfloor increasing the stability of the whole floor.

Personal Taste Prevails, but...

Mostly the choice in types of wooden flooring for each area is down to personal taste, but it is worth considering some points:

Long, narrow areas like hallways, will look even narrower and longer if a small full-plank with bevels is chosen. A better option here would be a 2 or 3-strip flooring where all the combined little strips, each with its own character, will focus ones view on the whole floor and not take your eye to the distant end of the lines.

Wider boards in large rooms will create an illusion of more space.

Staying with hallways, because of the heavy-traffic harder wood species are recommended for greater resistance against wear and tear. Light colours in these heavy-traffic areas will require a bit more maintenance, where a darker tone wouldn't show every speck of dirt as easily.

Two or 3-strips, due to their economical price compared with full-planks, and their varied character, will suite bedrooms. They can be a very cost-effective solution when an anti-allergic floor covering is needed, without compromising on variety of tones and textures.

The Importance of Colour

Colour is also a very important consideration. Don't forget that the colour of your walls and/or your lighting scheme (both natural and artificial) will also reflect on the wood.

Also, keep in mind that wood matures over time, meaning it will change in colour in a very natural way too. Oak, when a natural finish is applies, turns from pale to its typical Honey Colour, and many of the tropical species will turn darker. Request our special "All about the maturing of Wood-Species" leaflet, to see how over 20 different wood species will have changed colour in two years time.

Wooden Flooring Finish: Oil or Lacquer?

Question:
We would like to have our home layed with solid oak floor and are confused as to what finished product would suit us best, ie hard wax oil or lacquer. We have a 4 years old son who uses his plastic car to push around inside. Your advice as to which finish would be more resistance to scratch and last longer is much appreciated.

Answer:
In your circumstances we would recommend HardWaxOil every time. It's much more resilient, and if there are small damages it's much easier to repair locally than a varnished/lacquered floor.

One of the hardest questions to answer is: "What makes a better finish, lacquer or oil/HardWaxOil?"

History of Finishes

First of all, it's down to personal taste. Secondly, what is expected of the floor (e.g. easy maintenance, a shiny look or natural appearance of the wood).

Historically the wax floor is still seen as very labour intensive to maintain. Who doesn't have memories of people buffing away endlessly week after week after week (be it your Gran or the school caretaker). Then came the 'modern' lacquer (and synthetic, affordable, wall-to-wall carpets), and the original wax floor almost became extinct.

Lacquer

For many decades, most of the wooden flooring in the U.K. was pre-finished, lacquered, or lacquered/varnished on site. Maintenance became simple, buffing on hands and knees a thing of the past, and there was a choice between high gloss and matt appearances. The newest innovation in lacquer now has the same appearance as an oiled floor, to make the wood look more 'natural'.

The biggest **disadvantage of a lacquered finish** on a wooden floor is that it 'sits' on the floor.

When damaged with a sharp object, or due to the long term abrasive effect of dirt ('dirty' shoes 'sanding' away in heavy traffic areas, or under chairs, tables, etc.), the lacquer doesn't protect the wood any more. The dirt and moisture will make the wooden floor look 'grey', regardless of maintenance efforts. In fact, cleaning damaged areas with a moist cloth will make things worse.

The only proper solution would be to sand the complete floor and apply a new finish. Applying a proper lacquer layer is a job for the specialist, as lacquer is not very forgiving if mistakes are made.

Oil and Wax Floors

The labour intensive maintenance of the old-fashioned wax-floor has now become a thing of the past.

Oils replaced the many layers of wax. The oil penetrates the wood deeper than lacquer and makes it moist resistant, but still allows the wood to 'breathe'. A **hard wax** layer is applied afterwards to make the wear and tear layer water repellent.

HardWaxOil

Nowadays, most oiled floors are pre-finished (or finished on site) with **HardWaxOil**, which combines the natural oil (long term protection) and the carnauba or bees hard wax (wear and tear layer) in a two-in-one product. It's very easy to apply, and a very forgiving product when some mistakes are made. In fact, it's an ideal DIY-finish (although we still strongly recommend you read the instructions thoroughly, and use the right equipment!)

It has a great surface density, and is therefore very resistant to abrasive movements. Besides that, any (minor) damage is very easily repaired with some wax or maintenance oil, without the need to sand the whole floor.

The appearance of the finished wooden floor is matt satin, with the advantage of making the floor look warmer, and deeper in colour over the years.

Maintenance

An oiled-waxed or HardWaxOiled wooden floor requires slightly more maintenance than a lacquered floor, but not on the level of the old-fashioned knee and backbreaking wax floor. We have the modern maintenance products to thank for that.

On the other hand, wet shoe prints (think rain, Autumn, incoming traffic in hallways) don't show up immediately like they do on a varnished or lacquered floor.

Have we answered the question of what makes a better finish? No, sorry, we still can't. Ultimately it is still down to personal taste, we're afraid.

P.S: Personally our favourite finish is HardWaxOil on Oak and Euku oil on tropical... just so you know!

Before you begin - calculations, materials and tools

We're often asked what's the best adhesive, the best underlayment, or the best brand in wood flooring. Before we list those products and brands that we regularly use ourselves, and have good experiences with, it's worth adding a note of caution.

Materials can be a Help or a Hindrance.

Good quality products will assist you tremendously in getting the best results, or at least a decent one, and the old adage that "You get what you pay for" is absolutely true. Penny-pinch on important accessories like adhesive, underlayment, and even tools, and there is a high risk it will have a negative effect on the quality of your end result. At the very least it could cost you double the time it would normally take.

This doesn't mean you always have to buy the most expensive product around. Some alternative brands (or non-brands) will do an equal job to that of its "posh" relative. You have to decide what your situation needs as a maximum, and as a minimum requirement. A gentle sloping concrete floor could be screeded over, or you could carefully use extra underlayment to tackle the unevenness - more about this "trick" later. You could buy a professional jig-saw for around £400.00, but would you use it often enough after your floor is finished to justify the expense? Wouldn't a decent jig-saw of around £ 85.00 - £ 115.00 do the same job? Don't go too far though... a £ 25.00 budget jig-saw wouldn't do. You get the picture.

And **always, always** read the information on any tin, roll, tub, or bottle, **before** you buy - especially if you are not sure that it will do what you need it to do. An oil or varnish needs a bare wood surface and a room temperature between 16 - 23 degrees, a thin laminate underlayment will not give you the sound-insulation you want to reduce noise from an upstairs room fitted with wooden flooring, a 16kg tub of adhesive will not spread far enough to do an area of 25 sq m, etc.

In the same vein, PVAC wood-glue will not bond your floorboard to the underfloor, and nor will leaving an old carpet underlayment on the underfloor give you the best (and cleanest) base to install your wood floor upon. Yes, we've been asked!

How much Wood do you Need?

Calculating the amount of square meters you'll need depends on various items - the shape of your room, the amount of wood in a pack, whether you're installing in just one room or more, and sometimes even the quality of the product you buy.

Whatever your situation you have to add "saw-waste" to the calculation. Some will tell you to add 5%, others insist on 10%. Why "saw-waste" and how much?

1. To assist in the staggering of the pattern
2. To allow for the material you have to cut off in the last (and sometime also the first) row
3. To allow for cutting errors
4. To replace boards that have a blemish on them - one way or the other
5. To replace boards which nature decided to give a completely different colour or grain appearance than the rest of your floor
6. To allow for lining up floors in two connecting rooms (with or without the need or wish to install a threshold).

Rectangular rooms or bay-windows, fire-places, stairs etc?

Start with multiplying the width at the widest point with the longest length of your room. For L-shaped areas, like hallways, divide the area into rectangles and calculate the square meters per rectangle, then add up your total "raw" measurements. If there are obvious large areas you don't need wood for (the floor space a fireplace takes in for instance) subtract this from your raw measurements.

Now common sense comes into it. Adding 10% for saw-waste when you only plan to install a 4 sq meter hallway (4 meter long by 1 meter wide - i.e. 0.40 sq meters) wouldn't give you much room to manoeuvre, especially when for the last row you only need 1/4 width of the board (4 meter long x 3/4 width of the board "waste"). Say your installing 150mm wide boards, this would leave you with 0.44 saw-waste (cut off boards you have to buy but do not need).

In most circumstances we advice to add between 7 - 10% to your raw-measurements to give the total required sq meters of wood . If your preferred floor is packed per a certain amount of square meters, use common sense again. If your calculation tells you you need 6.1 pack and one pack contains 4.84 sq m (it happens!) you're left with an extra 4.35 sq meters for saw-waste if you purchase 7 packs. In these cases you have to decide if that 0.10 pack (0.48 sq meter in this scenario) is really needed based on the shape of the room etc. If you added 10%, change it to 8 or 9% and see where that brings you in regards of packs needed.

Kitchens
We want to add a special note for this room. Do you need to measure wall to wall or wall to kitchen units? Or in other words: installing the wood floor before or after the kitchen is installed (in those cases of course where you are revamping/building a whole new kitchen).

If the new wood floor doesn't replace your existing (load-bearing, installed directly onto joists) floor then our advice is:
measure from wall to just a bit underneath the kitchen units. Do not place your units onto your new floor. Wall to wall is in our opinion waste of material and money, plus in the event of a leak/flood you don't have to rip out your kitchen again to replace or repair your wood floor. Yes of course these disasters are covered by your insurance (we hope, did you check your policy lately?) but think of the extra hassle it will give!

Kitchen units are mostly 60cm x 60cm. So one unit is already 0.36 sq m, 3 units next to each other makes over 1 sq m of wood flooring you buy, install to never lay your eyes on again. Money we think you can use in better ways - especially when revamping a kitchen. It's better and more economical to install your wood floor about 5 to 10cm underneath the units and cut the kicking board to new height.

In areas where stand alone and not built-in utilities are planned, install plywood of the same height as your wood floor (including underlayment) so that when you need to move your washing machine, fridge or dish washer from its place (for whatever reason) you don't have to lift it up - just simply slide it from its plywood base onto the floor (take care not to damage your wood floor though).
Between plywood and wall and between plywood and wood floor you also have to keep an expansion gap which will be covered by the utility itself.

Brands and Products we can Recommend

In the *Preparations* section you'll find tips, and even some rules, on which type of products to use for glueing down, secret nailing and floating your floor - depending on your type of underfloor and other issues. See the *Preparing of your Underfloor* chapters for recommended products for these preparations.

Underneath we've listed the most common materials, accessories, and tools needed for the majority of jobs. It is unlikely to be a complete list, though, and there will always be something else you need! If you're in any doubt as to the suitability of products or methods in your unique situation, don't hesitate to email or phone for further advice.

We'll also publish this list on the *Recourse* webpage (www.woodmanuals.co.uk), so that when needed we can update it with new products available on the market.

Underlayment for Floating Installation

(Products are based on the presumption that your underfloor has been prepared correctly)

Level concrete underfloor without Underfloor Heating (UFH):
- "Combi-underlayment" or Barrier Plus 3mm (DPM + sound-insulation in one) 15 sq m per roll (1 meter wide).
- Timbermate Excel 3.6mm (DPM + better sound insulation in one) 10 sq m roll (0.685 x 14.6m), 15 sq m roll (1.37 x 1m). This underlayment weights rather a lot, so if you have to carry it upstairs, be warned!
- Elastilon self-adhesive underlayment (sound insulation, needs separate DPM sheet) Basic standard 3mm, Basic Sport 5 and 10mm - suitable for most solid floorboards and wood-engineered boards. Not suitable for narrow boards or nervous wood types like beech or pine boards (use Elastilon Strong for this). 50 sq m rolls - 1 meter wide (or cut to required sq m needed - at a price).

Existing floorboards, plywood, chipboard, OSB underfloor without UFH
- Foam underlayment or Barrier 3mm (sound-insulation) 15 sq m per roll - 1 meter wide.
- Timbermate Duratex 3.6mm (better sound insulation) 10 sq m roll (0.685 x 14.6m), 15 sq m roll (1.37 x 1m). This underlayment weights rather a lot, so if you have to carry it upstairs, be warned!
- Elastilon self-adhesive underlayment 3mm (sound-insulation).

Special underlayment for UFH
- Heatflow (Timbermate Duralay) 3mm, 15 sq m roll, 1 meter wide. Low thermal resistance level, 21db sound insulation.
- Elastilon Lock 2mm - warning from Elastilon manufacturer: Not intended for the layman or "cowboy-fitter", if you do not know exactly what you're doing (sorry). Self-adhesive on both sides becoming a fully integrated part of the under-floor heating system. 50 sq m roll -1 meter wide.

NOTE: 2mm foam underlayment from most DIYsheds is better (if at all) suitable for laminate floors, it's too thin and damages too easily to be useful. The 7mm fibreboards - also from most "sheds" - can give a bouncing feel to the wooden floor. If you need to tackle unevenness's of your underfloor, 7mm fibreboards are not going to do this for you - check the preparing your underfloor section for the correct ways.

Adhesives for Fully Bonding

(Products are based on the presumption that your underfloor has been prepared correctly).

Parquet floors: herringbone, basket weave, wood blocks, mosaic etc on all types of underfloors, (excluding modern chipboard), without UFH:
- Lecol5500 (16 kg),
- Lecol1630 beige and Lecol1633 brown (14 kg),
- F.Ball B92 Stycobond (7.5 and 15kg).

Usage - with the correctly notched trowel #3 - approximately 1200gr per sq m.

Floorboards on all types of underfloors, (excluding modern chipboard), with or without UFH, parquet floors on UFH:
- Mapei P990 (15kg),
- Sika T54 (15kg or sausages 600gr) - flexible adhesives.

Usages - with the correctly notched trowel #4 or #5 - floorboards, #3 parquet - appr. 1200 gr per sq m. Sika sausages have to be applied with special glue "gun" applicator.

Modern chipboard: can't be glued onto, due to its water repellent surface.

Products for Secret Nailing

Battens: at least 50mm (5 cm) high and preferably 75mm wide.
Hammer screws (for installing battens on concrete).
Nails: at least 50mm long (ribbed).

Check for any hidden pipe work or electrical cables **before** you start installing battens on any subfloor.

Do this also when you're removing existing floorboards from their joists, and need to saw through some of them. It wouldn't be the first time a plumber installed a (hot) water pipe in a small gap on the surface of a joist, instead of going underneath the joist as they should! Take especially good care when removing floorboards near doors, as pipes and cables are frequently installed very near the surface here.

Oils and HardWaxOils for Unfinished Floors

ONLY to be applied to unfinished floors. Never apply on a floor that still has a (residue) finish.

HardWaxOil:
* Blanchon natural or colours. You can tone down any of the colours by applying one coat of colour followed by one coat of natural. Available in 0.25, 1 and 2.5 lt (coverage: 1 lt per 10 sq m in two coats). Apply with a sponge, roller, or non-fluffy cloth. Always apply a second coat within 48 hours.
* Osmo Polyx (Hardwax) Oil matt or silk natural, available in 0.75, 2.5 or 10 lt (coverage: 1 lt per 10 sq m in two coats).
* Osmo Polix Oil Colour Foundation or Wood Wax Colour: apply before applying Osmo's natural Polyx Hardwax Oil. Available in 0.25, 0.75 (wood wax only) and 2.5 lt. Apply with a sponge, brush, or non-fluffy cloth.

Sealing Oils:
* Euku Oil 1, deep penetrating natural sealer (needs separate wear and tear layer, like wax or wax-polish). Available in 1, 3 and 5 lt. Apply with a sponge, woolen sleeve, or non-fluffy cloth.
* Oak and other European wood species - apply two coats, tropical species - apply one coat. Coverage: 1 lt per 30 sq m in one coat (1 lt per 15 sq m in two coats).
* Blanchon Wood Floor Oil Environment, natural or colour (2) - water based oil (needs separate wear and tear layer). Always apply 3 coats, and never wait longer than 48 hours between coats. Available in 1 and 3 lt (coverage: 1 lt per 15 sq m per coat = 1 lt per 5 sq m in three coats). Apply with short-hair roller.

For all oils and HardWaxOil the following should be followed after finishing: Never place rugs on the finished floor within 10 days. Spillages or water drips might create white marks (splashes) in the beginning (again within the 10 days the oils need to fully cure).

Side-note: From our earliest years we are "oil-people", and therefore cannot really recommend or advise on which varnishes and lacquers to use. However, Bona-Kemi, Blanchon and Lecol/Maiburg are well known for their high quality products in this regards.

Threshold and Beading

In other chapters/sections we cover why you should always treat every room as a separate entity. When you do this, and have two connecting rooms both with wood floors in them, you will need to cover the gap between the two floors in the doorway.

When we first arrived in the UK many years ago this was a new concept for us. In The Netherlands every (well, almost every) doorway has already a high and wide enough wooden threshold as part of the door frame. We would just leave the expansion gaps in front of this block of wood and cover the gap with a flat beading, job done. Here in the UK it is a different story, and we will list the most commonly used threshold solutions for each situation. Because there are so many different types and brands around we will only indicate the standard name of the threshold used. Some come with metal or plastic strip that need to be screwed down into the underfloor, and others come with a flat base that can be glued or pinned down. Unfortunately it is still rare to see a threshold and strip combination where you screw the threshold in the strip (counter sunk), which does make it easier to replace or adjust. Perhaps one day the manufacturer of these type of sturdy thresholds will manage to find the UK!

From wood to wood at same level:
Use either a T-bar or a wide flat strip which is bevelled on both sides. The T-bar rests its base on the underfloor (either directly or in a metal bar provided with the T-bar). The wide strip only sits on the wood floor and is pinned to one or both floors on either side of the doorway. The wide strip has the advantage of not having to have a very wide gap between the two floors, because at both sides of the base of the T-bar you will have to leave your calculated expansion gap.

From wood to carpet or vinyl:
Normally the wood will end up higher than the carpet. You can use either a Ramp or a Reducer.
What's the difference? Well, a Ramp has a flat base running to the lowest end of the threshold, where the Reducer has a smaller base and a lip at the lowest end.
A Reducer is also ideal to use when you go from wood to wood at another level.

From wood to tiles:
If the wood is higher than the tiles - use a so-called End or L-threshold. In many cases the tiles are not level - think of the grouting in between the tiles - which would make any other threshold "rock" or wobble and lose its fixing.

If the wood is lower than the tiles - cover the expansion gap with a flat beading which has a bevelled edge (so you have a gentle transition between wood and the beading). The same goes for fire-places or fire-surrounds: Wood higher, use an end, wood lower, use flat beading.
Ends are also commonly used around a mat well.

Expansion gap covers:
You can choose between Scotia, Quadrants or Flat Beading of the same wood type as your floor (or unfinished so you can stain/colour it in the same colour) - which we prefer because it makes a neat and simple finish.

Scotia and Quadrants are attached to the skirting board and the floor moves underneath it. Flat beading is attached (pinned) to the wood floor and moves with the floor. Because it moves with the floor (and you can regard it as an early warning system there is movement) you should use tiny pins (or brads) which are easily lifted up out of the beading when the floor expands. One of the advantages of flat beading is that you can install it (almost) everywhere, even where there are no skirting boards (patio-doors etc).

When radiator-pipes come out of the floor you have to leave a gap around them too. There are solid wood radiator-pipe-covers, which are available in many sizes and wood-species, and pre- or unfinished to cover this gap in a neat way.

Top of stairs (when installing a wood floor on landing)
solid Oak stair nosings come in various shaped and sizes, some (ours) even as a two part construction. Make sure whatever nosing you use the wood on the landing has room to move. So products that have to be laid flush with your wood floor could cause problems later.

With all wooden materials please note: Each is a product of nature with its own character and colouring. Thresholds, beading, and other covers, can also come from a different origin than your wood floor (for instance European Oak floor, and American Oak threshold). This can result in colour differences including different reactions when staining or colouring them.

Other Materials to Have Handy

Additional materials that have proven to be very handy to have close by:

Hardboard sheets in various thicknesses.
These can be used to cut into strips to assist you where the floor dips a little bit, or to build up a gentle slope that effects the movement of your floor. When you use hardboard strips (or extra underlayment) to fill a little dip you hadn't noticed before you started the installation NEVER lift the board to insert the extra material, as this will result in the underfloor becoming more uneven the other way around. Slide the strip of underlayment beneath it, and when it's stuck it's gone as far as it wants or needs to go -

so don't force it further. If you do, you'll regret it rows and rows later when you suddenly realise there is a bounce in the floor.

Cloths: For wiping off spilled PVAC glue from your hands, underlayment, wood floor etc. Just keep the cloth tucked in to your waistband - because the minute you leave it on the floor it has the tendency to disappear or become out of reach just when you most need it! Cloths must be distantly related to pencils - another item that have this unexplained tendency to disappear into thin air!

Tools

Remember what we said at the beginning of this section: Decent quality tools will do most of the tricks. If you are a frequent DIY-er, your shed may already be full of all the tools you need. If you're a beginner, or have never attempted DIY-jobs that require wood working tools, you can purchase many decent tools at most DIY-sheds. If you think this will be a job you'll only do once, it's also possible to hire the majority of the tools. There's no need to purchase professional tools - they are more expensive because they need to be of higher quality to sustain the punishment of regular or consistent use.

For all installation methods:
- Jigsaw - with variable speed, precision control and splinter guard. (Cordless saws that can do the trick are rather expensive). Purchase (and use) suitable blades too.
- Hand saw.
- Stanley (type) knife with spare blades.
- Knocking block.
- Jemmy bar.
- Work bench (or sturdy toolbox) for (presicion) cutting that should not be done out of the hand.
- Tape-measure. (make sure it's long enough).
- Pencils (loads!).
- Ruler.
- Spirit-level.
- Hammer.
- Heavy duty bin bags.

Other tools - if you have them in your shed, or they are simple to hire in. You can do without them, but they can make some parts of the job easier:
- Chop-saw with slide.
- Tacker (for brads).

"Special" tools for **glueing** a floor down:
- Notched trowel.
- Cleaning product for your tools, (and your hands!) according to instructions of the adhesive supplier.

"Special" tools for **secret nailing**:

- Porta (type) nailer.
- Powerful drill (for installing batten on concrete floors).

As you can read - there's no mention of screws anywhere. If, in the end, there is movement in your floor, screwing it down is **not** the solution! It might temporarily solve your movement issues, but when the floor starts to go through its natural seasonal movement (or extreme movement caused by whatever reason) the screw will prevent the normal movement and create more problems.

Side-note: If you bought a wooden floor that comes with its own specific special screws, then you have to follow the instructions of the manufacturer. We are still not convinced that screws will work in wooden floors, no matter who invented them, but in order to keep the warranty of your floor valid you must follow their instructions.

PREPARATIONS

Preparations

Schedule works in the right order

Question:
I'm getting plasterers in to do a skim coat on all of my walls next week. When they are finished I intend to put down pine floorboards in the same rooms. Can I start the 2-week acclimatisation for the floorboards now - or should I wait until the plaster is fully dry? ie. will the moisture from the drying plaster adversely affect the wood?

Answer:
Yes it will.
After the plastering is done ventilate the room(s) more then you would do normally, to allow the excess moisture to escape to the outside world. At the moment (winter 2004) the air humidity is low which will help you.

Wet and Dusty First

During renovations, or redecoration, a lot of work has to be done. Cabling, plumbing, screeding, plastering, wall-papering, painting, and so on. When you also plan to have a new wooden floor installed, it's very important to schedule this job as a final task.

Basically, you first need to do all the 'wet-work' in and around the room(s) where you plan to lay wooden flooring, and allow sufficient time for the excess moisture from plastering and/or painting to evaporate.

An Example of Wrong Order, or Bad Planning

We gave the BBC's DIY-SOS team the same advice when we were asked if it would be possible for us to install one of our quality wooden floors for them at short notice.

The short notice wasn't the problem, nor was the fact that we would have just one day to install it. The problem was that there was going to be a lot of plastering and painting in the days immediately before.

You really shouldn't install a wooden floor (wood-engineered included) the day after you have just finished plastering or painting.

Since the DIY-SOS program is always working on a very tight time-schedule, we advised the team to source another type of floor-covering. Of course, in the future we would be more than happy to help them out - as long as their project doesn't involve massive plaster work beforehand!

In renovation projects like this it's useful to have a hygrometer handy in the room where you're working, as a guide to when the moisture from plastering and painting is gone. You can speed this process up with sufficient ventilation, so that the excess moisture in the air is drawn out of the room - even in winter. Just open the windows for 5 - 10 minutes every hour.

For screed work (or new concrete) there is a useful and practical 'rule of thumb': For every inch (2.5 cm) of screed/concrete you'll need to allow 30 days for it to dry-out naturally before any floor-covering (but especially wooden floors) can be installed. Any less, and it could cause you problems with expansion or cupping straight away. The moisture in the screed/concrete should be around 2% - 2.5% tops before you can start the installation of a wooden floor.

When you install a wooden floor on an underfloor that's still too wet, trust us... you'll notice this pretty soon. The wood will absorb the moisture of the screed/concrete (even when a combi-underlayment is installed) and expand very quickly.

So be patient, and prepare your 'when-to-do-what' task list very carefully, but practically.

Better safe than sorry.

Reclaimed Floors

Special consideration to planning should be given here. Your reclaimed floorboards, or wood blocks, should be as clean as possible and have most if not all the bitumen (tar) removed from them. If not, you run the risk that the adhesive will take many days, instead of just overnight, to properly bond your floor.

Don't underestimate the time this can take. Plan ahead and build enough time into your schedule to tackle this not so nice job. Or be aware of what you buy, and if you have the option to buy cleaned blocks or floorboards then decide if that's worth the extra money versus your own time. (Do check the condition of these clean floors though, as if it was agreed the bitumen was fully removed don't accept anything less than just a stained surface and clean grooves).

The simplest trick to remove bitumen yourself (if we're talking blocks that is) is to place them in a freezer, which will make the bitumen brittle and easier to chisel off. But it is a dirty job. Sanding off with a simple belt sander will only clog up the paper within seconds. Some DIY-ers report good results with a planer or bench saw, but this only works when the blocks are thick - at least 20mm - and make sure you use the equipment in such a way that you can't hurt yourself!

And Don't Forget to Acclimatise your Floor!

When you buy your wood floor, you're never sure where it has been stored by the merchant, timber yard, DIY-shed or retailer. Outside? In a storage facility without climate control? Wood is a product of nature and will adapt to its surroundings - giving enough time to do so.

When your floor is supplied and has a rather high moisture content, you're asking for trouble when you install the boards on the same day or week as they arrive at your home. The excess moisture will "evaporate" to the air and your wood will shrink.

So allow your wood floor to really acclimatise to your home climate. For solid floors this can take up to 4 - 5 weeks, depending where it comes from. For wood-engineered boards this is normally around 3 - 4 days.
This means adding the job of getting the wood in your home on time to your schedule. Somewhere at a point where, when stored, the wet works still to be done or in progress don't have an effect on the acclimatising! Most wood floors come in packs which can be stacked onto each other behind a sofa, along a wall in your dining, bedroom or study etc. You get the picture, stack your wood there where there is no risk of it being damaged by your normal 'traffic' nor by your "work-in-progress".

Always leave the floor in the packaging it came in, and don't remove the wrapping or carton boxes. It is not needed to help with the acclimatisation, but you risk damaging the boards unnecessary when moving it around.

It's always best to store the wood floor in the room it is planned to be installed in, as this way your floor adapts to the normal climate in that room prior for installation. You can imagine a hallway having a different temperature as your living room, and your kitchen a higher humidity than your study. We won't mention that garages or sheds are a definite no no - you are, we're sure, intelligent enough to realise that it's not a place to acclimatise your wood floor.

And perhaps we also shouldn't mention this, but we have seen it happening: All your outside walls and windows should already by in place, to make your room wind and weather tight of course, otherwise your wood floor will acclimatise to the circumstances of the outside world!

Other Precautions

Oh, and while we're at it - make sure there is enough light available, even if you plan to install the floor during day-light hours only. It could be a very dark and cloudy day.

Your foundation for the best result: the Underfloor

[Extra info available online - www.woodmanual.co.uk]

Question:
We've just built a new house and have had the heating on for the past number of weeks. We tested the moisture level of the concrete the flooring will go on and it's currently 4%. The wood for the floor has been in the house for the past 2 weeks. Would we be ok to go ahead and lay the flooring now?

Answer:
You'll have to wait a bit longer we're afraid. The moisture level in the concrete should be 2% or less before you can install the wood floor. Rule of thumb: every inch (2.5 cm) of concrete/ screed takes approximately 30 days to dry.

Check the type of underfloor you have before you begin purchasing your materials. The type of underfloor will determine which kind of underlayment you need.

Concrete Floors

IMPORTANT: New concrete or screed needs 30 days for every inch (2.5 cm) of depth to dry out sufficiently, before installation of any floor covering can take place. Never force dry a concrete floor, as this might cause cracks which could crumble further or let through moisture. Make sure the surface of the concrete/screed is level.

On dry concrete/screed use DPM* plus sound-insulation. Increasingly this is sold as a 2 in 1 product, with handy self-adhesive overlapping strip of DPM.

* DPM stands for Damp Proof Membrane

The DPM layer prevents any residue moisture from the concrete getting into the wood. It's not really needed on concrete underfloors on second floors, but it won't hurt.

The attached foam layer acts as a sound-insulation, preventing your real wooden floor sounding like a Melamine Laminate floor, and has the ability to 'fill' some minor unevenness in the underfloor.

You should also use a combi-underlayment when the existing floor covering - you can't or don't want to remove - is made of vinyl or plastic (Marley) tiles. This floor covering can start to 'sweat' when covered up and the DPM on the combi-underlayment will prevent the moisture of this getting into your wood floor.

Existing Floorboards, Plywood or Chipboard

DON'T use DPM.
The reason for not using a DPM when installing onto existing floorboards is that this would block the normal ventilation that should be present underneath the existing floorboards (the void which should have air gaps in the walls). Any moisture that normally evaporates harmlessly through the boards into the air will be trapped against the DPM and might cause rotting of the existing floorboards and even your joists.

Using a normal foam underlayment in these cases makes sure the moisture - every home has more or less moisture during the seasons - will still be able to evaporate through the whole construction. When your underfloor is level a 2-3mm foam is sufficient. If you need more sound-insulation it's best to use a thicker underlay.

When you have a old fashion parquet floor (5 finger mosaic etc) which you can't or don't want to remove, you need to use a foam underlayment too - even if the mosaic was originally stuck down on a concrete floor. Using a DPM will prevent any moisture from the concrete to evaporate naturally and could cause the wood of your old underfloor to rot.

So in fact it is quite easy to remember:
- Installing directly onto concrete, screed or "plastic": underlayment with DPM.
- For everything else: underlayment without DPM.

Whatever kind of underlayment you need, don't be a cheapskate with the materials you use. It'll cost you more in the end (inferior materials = more time correcting, plus the end result of your natural real wooden floor could sound like a 'plastic' Melamine Laminated floor).

Different types of Underfloors in one area

When you have one area containing two (or more) types of underfloor, you have to start with other preparations - making sure you have one type of underfloor.

For example: You have an extension with a new concrete underfloor, connected to a room which has existing floorboards. Both types of underfloor can have a different temperature or moisture content, and your natural wooden floor will react accordingly. One part of a board when laid across both types could 'go-all-over-the-place' and you could end up with a cupped or warped floor. The simplest solution in this situation is to install plywood, or OSB, sheets over the whole area. Then use stainless steel screws for large sheets, or glue (flexible adhesive) for small sheets (30 x 60cm maximum) to the concrete, and nail or staple sheets onto the existing floorboards. Install the sheets in a diagonal direction so that there is no risk of ending a row of sheets exactly on the border between the two types of underfloors. If both areas are fairly level you can substitute the plywood or OSB with 3 - 6mm hardboard sheets.

On the plywood/OSB/hardboard (sheet material) use a foam or rubber underlay for sound-insulation and your underfloor is ready for the wooden floor.

If you use the glueing down method you can use one type of adhesive when you create one type of underfloor. For secret nailing a wood floor, other criteria matter - especially the thickness of the underfloor/subfloor your nails have to pass through. We will cover this in more detail in the chapter about secret nailing.

A question frequently asked about this is "Should I install a DPM first on the concrete before creating one type of underfloor using hardboard, plywood or OSB?" Well, not really. If you use large sheets (standard 8" x 4"), the screws you use will render the DPM useless anyway, and flexible adhesives when glueing sheets down to concrete will work as a DPM anyway. Of course, only do this after you've made sure your concrete is dry enough.

Height Difference in/between Rooms/Area's - Knocking Down Walls

Almost no underfloor is truly level. You can and will always encounter some height differences or slopes. With concrete floors these, typically, can be found near walls or (patio) doors where the level often goes up. As long as the slope is not more than 3mm per meter (in one direction) most wooden floorboards can tackle this difference without creating hollow sound effects or movement. Of course, the thicker your board, the fewer problems you have - a 10mm wood-veneer or laminate will flex easier than 15 or 20mm boards.
If the slope is steeper, or in more directions, you have to solve this first to prevent movement in your wood floor. Please don't think adhesive can be used as filler - it can't. The result will be that parts of the board will not bond with the adhesive, creating hollows, and will flex or move when walking over it. See the chapters on preparing the underfloor for more details on how to solve this.

Most problems occur when you knock two rooms into one by removing a wall - after first making sure it is not a load bearing wall, of course! Often both old rooms have their individual underfloors which could differ in height. You'll need to make good any significant difference, especially if the wall was small - because the steep slope would be too much for any board to handle. Sometimes it's only the transition between the rooms that needs filling up or knocking down, until both underfloors have the same level. Larger height differences can be tackled by adding hardboard, or even plywood, to one of the rooms. Note, it's always best to stay away from chipboard, this will limit your installation methods.

Preparing a Sub-floor or Underfloor

Question:
In that I am totally inexperienced at this, I humbly engage your patience. Would I need to remove the old flooring before laying the new or could I do a layover? My house was built in 1911; the panels have not been changed since the origination Thank you

Answer:
If your existing floorboards are level (un-cupped and sound) you can install your new floor on top of it without any problems. We recommend you use a foam underlayment for sound-insulation, leave expansion gaps all around of min. 10mm

(Part Guest Article by Matty Bourne - BwfA)

All proper installations start with checking the state of your subfloor or underfloor, to determine if it needs any work done to first. Below you'll find the most common underfloor types, and in the event that these are not sound or level enough for your wooden floor to be installed on, there are tips and advice on how to correct this.

Wooden Sub-floor

Floorboards. You'll need to use a long straight edge to determine how smooth your floorboards are. If they are reasonably smooth, i.e. 1-2mm deviation, you should over board with an exterior grade 6mm plywood. If you have bad cupping of the boards you'll need to step up the thickness of plywood to bridge across the cupped boards, for example to 12mm or more. Alternatively sand the cupped boards flat and go back to using the 6mm plywood.

Chipboard. This type of sub floor should be over boarded with minimum 6mm plywood, as secret nailing and glueing down is almost impossible to do on a chipboard underfloor.

How to install plywood
Plywood should first be left to acclimatise in the area to be prepared for a minimum of 48hrs. To fix the plywood to the sub floor it needs to be stapled with divergent staples, nailed with ring shank nails, or screwed down. Always fix the boards working from the centre out wards. You staples, nails, etc., every 25 cm, but no more than 1 cm from the edge. You should leave 5mm gaps (the thickness of a credit/deibt card) between the board joints.

Concrete/Screed

Use a long straight edge to determine the dips and high spots of the sub floor. Any high spots should be ground down. Any low spots should be marked out on the sub floor, and if the dips in the base are deeper than 3mm they should be filled with repair compound. All sub floors must be primed! Next you need to apply a suitable leveling compound. All compounds should be laid at a minimum of 3mm thickness and no deeper than 6mm. Mix all compounds as instructed on the bag.

Which smoothing/levelling compound should I use?

- Water based: Has especially good leveling and flow, and dries to a very hard surface. The down side is that it's not forgiving with mistakes when mixing, with damp, or poor priming. These will result in failure.
- Acrylic based: Dries to a very hard surface, and it's difficult to make mistakes in the mixing. The negative side is that it doesn't flow as well as water based compounds.
- Latex based: Easy to mix and very forgiving, but not as strong as other compounds. It also has poor shear strength, and doesn't flow very well.
- Water based flex: Designed for problem floors which flex. It can be used over floorboards. The down side is the price, and it must be kept more than 3mm deep.

Testing for sub floor moisture.

To meet British Standards, the amount of moisture in a concrete base you wish to lay a floor on, must not be more than 75% relative to humidity. To test this you need a working damp proof membrane, and a cured concrete base if new. The test should be done with a hygrometer - a box, which is then sealed to the floor for an average of 48-72hrs. Different mixes and depths take different times to generate a reading, so more than one area of the sub floor must be tested. Remember - new concrete will need at least a month per inch to dry! So 6" needs 6 months drying time!!

(Note from *Wood You Like*: other moisture measuring equipment (tested and approved to be used for floor installation preparations), different to the above mentioned, measures the percentage of moisture content in the screed. If this type of equipment is used the reading should not exceed 2% moisture content.)

Surface epoxy DPM.

If your underfloor has a failed damp proof membrane, or no damp proof protection at all, you can install an epoxy coat to act as a surface damp proofer. This will work up to about 92% relative to humidity (or up to 4% moisture content), depending on which product is used. You can also use a surface membrane to fast track fitting your new flooring on new concrete sub floors. Make sure you follow instructions supplied with the product you choose.

Weakest Links and Brands to Use

If you plan to glue down your wooden floor on to a concrete underfloor, be aware that the bonding of the adhesive with both the underfloor and your wood floor is the most important aspect of this method. If one or both fail, your whole floor fails.

Use and follow the advice given above by Matt Bourne to make sure there is no weak link in your underfloor. As for which brand to use, for primer or screed, ask the supplier/manufacturer of your adhesive which product they recommend. Most have their own range of preparation products that are tried and tested in conjunction with their other products, like adhesive.

Dusty concrete/screed needs to be treated with a primer too when you plan to glue down your floor, as the dust will prevent the adhesive from bonding properly with the concrete/screed. Don't take a chance with this, as even after vacuum cleaning the dust can still be present. You have to take proper action first. Again, check with the supplier of your adhesive what type or brand they recommend.

Floor Preparations over Bitumen

Question:
Hi. A little advice please.
I am laying a solid wood floor in my hall. But first I need to rip up the parquet flooring which is no good and the floor itself is not level. The parquet floor has been fixed to the floor by bitumen.

Any advice would be appreciated on which type of floor levelling screed/compound to put over the bitumen. Would I need to seal in the bitumen as to ensure the levelling compound adheres???

Many thanks

(Guest article by Matty Bourne - BwfA)

Bitumen was the product most commonly used to 'glue' parquet and other flooring to concrete in the 50's, 60's and 70's. It is a black, tar-like substance - officially a residue product from oil refineries - which gets brittle over time. It's always best to remove the bitumen from the underfloor to prevent problems later.

Problems can vary between loosening of the new blocks of boards - due to the fact you effectively only glued the new wood floor to the brittle bitumen - to creaking sounds when loose bits of the old bitumen are stuck between new floor and old concrete floor.

How to Remove Bitumen (tar) from an Existing Concrete Floor

Question: "Is there any way we can screed over bitumen when we want to glue a wooden floor down?"

Answer: The bitumen should always be removed and not screeded over. The sub floor SHOULD be shot blasted to remove all bitumen and glue residue.

I prime with a neoprime primer and use acrylic leveling compound over the top ONLY if the Bitumen is well stuck down and very thin. This will give you a good flat base. You can then use a epoxy DPM paint to deal with any moisture problems.

Please remember that this is NOT a recommended method by the product manufacturers. You are relying on how well the bitumen paint is stuck to the sub floor!

Do not use a latex flooring smoothing compound! These compounds are good for nothing, and normally used by people who have no idea (i.e. 95% of builders). They will stick to anything you put them over but have very little strength, so basically you can NOT use a epoxy compound or any sort of glue over the top!

Matt Bourne (BwfA)

Solid Floors - What to Note and Why
[Extra info available online - www.woodmanual.co.uk]

Question:
I intend laying t+g oak boards onto a dining room floor (floating method). However, the dining room leads into the kitchen. Would 20mm x 120mm oak boards be suitable in the kitchen if properly finished and sealed? If yes, the concrete floor they'd be laid onto sits above a dry cellar. Would you still recommend an underlay with DPM? Many thanks

Answer:
With kitchens we normally recommend wood-engineered boards - they are more stable in areas with more moisture. We do recommend installing a combi-underlayment in the kitchen to prevent any residue moisture from the concrete getting into the wood. The dry cellar can cause a colder climate underneath, with possible - on occasions - condensation. The DPM will help prevent problems caused by this.

Solid hardwood floors have been around for many years. However, more and more manufacturers are switching to wood-engineered floors for various - good - reasons.

This chapter will highlight issues you have to note when purchasing and installing solid wood floors, to make sure you end up with the best results possible

Recommended Measurements of Solid Floorboards and some Important Rules

Rule of thumb: The width of a solid board should never be wider than 10 times the thickness of the board.

So 20mm thick means a maximum of 200mm wide, 15mm thick means 150mm wide maximum.

'Oversized' boards are very prone to buckle and cup.

Rule of thumb: The location of the *tongue* and *groove* should be as close to the centre as possible to give the board the best stability. Sold floors with the tongue and groove below the centre are prone to buckle and cup.

The reason usually given for why the tongue and groove is almost at the bottom of the board is that the floor can be sanded many more times. Whilst this might sound valid, running the risk of cupped boards before there is ever a need to have the floor sanded outweighs this 'benefit' many times over.

Rule of thumb: Solid floors can be installed floating if:
- They are wider than 100mm
- The room is not wider than 5 - 6 meters
- and in cases with random length: maximum 15% of the boards are of 'short' lengths (see below: "Short end of the stick").

Rule of thumb: Overall, solid floorboards will expand and shrink more than wood-engineered boards. To allow this movement you need to calculate the correct expansion gap required (and don't fill this gap with cork or anything else!).

Oak floors: For every meter width of the room, leave a 4mm gap - with a **minimum of 10mm**. A two meter wide area means a 10mm gap; a 3 meter wide room needs a 12mm expansion gap.

Make sure your skirting board are thick enough to cover the movement of shrinkage as well - we recommend 18 - 21 mm thick skirting for solid floors.

Pine boards: 4 - **5mm** per meter.

Beech -   A rather 'nervous' wood type - floors: **7mm** per meter.

Rule of thumb: Moisture content of a solid oak floorboard must be between 8 - 11% when it arrives in your home. Leave solid floors to acclimatise to your house climate (in their packaging) for at least 2 - 3 weeks if they are supplied by a reputable company. (Of course, you may never know where your floor has been stored if you buy via Ebay!)

Take note in which season you are installing the floor:
Winter - When your house climate is rather dry due to central heating effect, add 2mm extra to your calculated expansion gap.
Late summer/autumn - When your house climate has a high humidity, your floor will shrink more when the heating season starts. This is a normal effect, but don't reduce the standard expansion gap for this reason. It's better to add 2mm to your skirting board thickness (if you need to buy new ones - alternatively use flat beading to cover expansion gaps and leave skirting boards in situ).

General advice: Keep the width of solid boards narrow - 150 - 160mm tops - for the best, trouble free result. If you fancy a wider board then select wood-engineered, which is a much safer bet, and in the end looks exactly the same. You only see the surface of your solid wood floor - and the top layer of wood-engineered floors are definitely solid wood!

What Solid 'Offers' can be - If You're Not Careful

When you search the Internet (or your local paper for that matter) you can easily find many cheap offers for solid oak wood flooring.

Before buying into these offers, there are a few things you should be aware of:

Short lengths. Many of these offers contain over 75% short lengths (between 30 to 50cm) instead of a regular mix between short, medium, and long lengths (or fixed length of minimum 1.5 meter). Many short boards means many joints, all acting as hinges which makes your floor rather "unstable".

Difference in width. Really cheap offers are nothing more than bought up 'left-overs' from pallets. Sizes per pallet can vary, even if the packaging tells you differently. Some minor differences between the boards (0.5 - 1mm) doesn't effect the installation that much, but when you end up with a mix of boards all having a different, slightly off average width, you'll end up with one big jig-saw puzzle - and nothing will fit tightly together. Imagine one row of three meters with three different widths (board A is 110mm, board B is 109mm, and board C is 111mm). The next row has two boards (one 109mm and one 111mm). The first board in row two connects with boards A and B in row one, but because there is already a difference in width between the boards in row one, row two will never fit tightly... and so on and so on.

Remember: You get what you pay for. We have seen results of these cheap offers, coming from open sheds where temperature and moisture/humidity control isn't one of the priorities of the seller.

Beware of the 'Short End of the Stick'

Wood flooring is a very popular floor covering. Besides being easy to clean and anti-allergic, it enhances your home and can even increase the value of it.

But.... being popular has its own down-sides. Many are jumping on the 'band-wagon' of its success to make a profit. Nothing wrong with this when quality products are offered for what they are worth, but we all know and understand the logic of 'value for money'.

"Value for money" not only means **supplying decent products** but also **supplying decent information**, correctly and honestly. That is sometimes the biggest problem with 'Solid Offers' - too little information on what the "offer" really contains. The above picture - see the extra info online - was kindly supplied to us by one of *DIYnot.com* forum members. Besides problems with the pre-oiled finish, and installation errors by the fitter (not the forum-member), the floor has many very short lengths and hardly any longer lengths.

Products like these (most with a proper finish) are sold as Solid Oak floorboards - oak strip flooring - in random lengths between 300 - 1200mm (we "fondly" call these products "Master's Choice"). The correct and honest information **missing in the shop, and on the packaging,** is the amount of short lengths a pack contains. Sometimes as much as **50%** of the contents of a pack are **shorter than 400mm,** and only 1 or 2 boards - if you're lucky - are the full 1200mm long.

Rule of thumb: If random lengths are offered, only 15% maximum should be short - where short means 1/4 length of the longest length. In the case described here this would mean 15% of the boards are allowed to be short - 300mm minimum (1/4 of 1200mm) - **NOT 50%**!

Since it is recommended to prevent a pattern of joints, and to space the joints of connecting rows at least 300mm apart, this amount of short lengths makes it very hard to do. You create an unstable floor, that's prone to movement - see picture above - because of the many joints. None of the short lengths can be "sandwiched" between longer boards in neighbouring rows to counter-act this.

You will end up with a 'hinged' floor - one very good reason not to install a product like this using the floating method.

It can also give your solid oak real wood floor a very hectic appearance, especially if all 4 sides are bevelled. This makes the many joints in the floor even more pronounced.

Value for money: **If the information on the packs leaves you in doubt, ask the supplier for specifications.** They ought to know what he or she is selling you in the first place!

Don't end up with the **"short end of the stick"...** or in these cases "short end of the boards"!

INSTALLATION
OF
FLOORBOARDS

Installation of floorboards: the basics

Which Direction and how to Tackle More Rooms
[Extra info available online - www.woodmanual.co.uk]

Question:
I am doing my first wood floor. Everything checks out as far as flooring tools etc. My question is where to start the flooring. The room has three walls. The open side leads into the kitchen and two of the three walls have door connecting other rooms. My first thought it to start at the open side that leads into the kitchen. If so do I top nail the first board or use the floor nailer?
I appreciate any advice!

Answer:
Starting at the open side is a good idea. Then you are sure there is one full plank where the room starts (from the kitchen point of view). Try to avoid a joint in the middle of the opening - if possible of course. Is there a step between the room and the kitchen? If not, make sure you leave the correct expansion gap for the first row too.

Depending on the underfloor you could nail blocks of wood to a sheet material underfloor (or the existing floorboards) to act as a fixation point. This also forces you to create that important expansion gap. If you have a different situation than I imagine please let me know and I can advice/help with other tips.

Every room is different. Some are square, some rectangular, and some even round or octagonal. In which direction to install your floorboards is subject to various criteria.

Most Common Options

In most cases floorboard are installed parallel to the longest wall.

It's also usual to install them "with the light" - where the windows are located at the shortest wall(s) of a room. This way the grain of the wood will show its 'best side', and with bevelled floors false shades are prevented.

Most Practical Alternatives

The above options are not set in stone. Sometimes the specific dimensions of a room require a different approach, for example, in conservatories. Then it's best to install in a way that is most aesthetically pleasing - and make sure the bevels of your boards are not too pronounced (none or micro-bevels would be the best option).

If in doubt, install a few boards "dry", and move them in various directions while taking a step back to see which direction looks and feels the most aesthetically pleasing in that particular room.

Thresholds Between Rooms?

Mostly - Yes: With floorboards (solid or wood-engineered) treat every room separately, and install (wooden) thresholds in between. Every room has its own climate - a hallway is normally colder than your lounge, or a "next-door" dining room which you don't use often.
This also gives you the option to change direction in various rooms (see above).

With design parquet, different "rules" apply.

Another rule of thumb concerning "open" areas: As long as the opening is at least 3/5th of the wall in between you can treat the area as one and don't need to install a threshold.

Expansion Gaps - Very Important for the Best Results

Question:
Hi, Regarding expansion gaps, given that the amount of expansion is very weather dependent, presumably if the "standard" gap is 10mm then I'd leave this if installing the floor during a dry period mid winter, but leave very little gap (3-4mm?) if installing during a humid period in midsummer and pro-rata the gap in between? Or is there any other rule of thumb to ensure that the floor edges don't appear from under the skirting board in midwinter after I've installed in mid summer? Thanks

Answer:
There is a rule of thumb indeed: with solid Oak floors it's 3mm per meter width of the room, with a minimum of 10mm. In humid installation conditions leave at least 10mm, never narrower and install 18 - 21mm thick skirtingboards on top. For wood-engineered boards leave 10mm, and you can use thinner skirtingboards: 15 - 18mm thick

This is one of those items that, when overlooked, will come back to haunt you. No matter how well, or how professionally, you are able to install your wooden floor - forget this, and your floor will "take revenge" sometime soon!

Gaps Everywhere!

We start with repeating the rule of thumbs:
Overall, solid floorboards will expand and shrink more than wood-engineered boards. To allow this movement you need to calculate the correct expansion gap required (and don't fill this gap with cork or anything else!).

Oak floors: For every meter width of the room, leave a 4mm gap - with a **minimum of 10mm**. A two meter wide area means a 10mm gap; a 3 meter wide room needs a 12mm expansion gap.

Make sure your skirting board are thick enough to cover the movement of shrinkage as well - we recommend 18 - 21 mm thick skirting for solid floors.

Pine boards: 4 - **5mm** per meter.

Beech - A rather "nervous" wood type - floors: **7mm** per meter.

Lately we've seen (DIY) forum posts, questions in our own inbox, and even results by diy-ers and builders alike, about not leaving enough expansion gaps when installing wooden floors.

Most know about gaps, and leaving them around the perimeter of the floor using the simple rule of thumb: 3-4mm per meter width of the room with a minimum of 10mm.

But they then go wrong at certain points in rooms or hallways, or with the direction the floorboards are laid. In those occasions where you install parallel to the shortest wall, the "width" of your floor is the total length of the longest wall! Therefore, in a room measuring 6m x 3m, where the boards are installed parallel to the shortest wall (the 3m wall), you calculate the expansion gap based on the 6 meter width - i.e. at least 24mm, not 12mm for Solid Oak floors.

You have to leave expansion gaps **ALL AROUND** the perimeter of the whole floor, not just here and there, or where you can cover the gap with skirting boards. If you don't have a sufficiently wide expansion gaps in any one place, such as a doorpost, or in front of the fireplace or staircase, all the other expansion gaps which are wide enough will be rendered useless! Your wood floor is not going to think: "Oh, there's not a gap so I won't expand there." Believe me, it will!

And don't forget to leave an expansion gap around radiator-pipes coming through your wood floor too! It's known - we've seen it for ourselves - that expanding floors snap the pipe and cause a leak or flood.

A wood floor, especially a solid wood floor, will expand evenly. That's true in most cases, but when it's stuck at one certain point, it can't. It will raise its level at, or around, the point that is blocking its normal movement. For instance when glue has dripped out of the tongue and groove joints, and sticks the wood floor to the underlayment.

The same can occur when you haven't undercut your doorpost, or laid the floor flush against the side of a fireplace or staircase. There are always excuses… "The skirting board doesn't reach that far." "I don't know what to cover the gap with around the fire place." "I don't like to use a divider between the rooms where the wood floor is installed in two different directions anyway."

But we can't change the laws of physics – it's as simple as that!

Leave expansion gaps all around the perimeter. There are various solutions – proper, aesthetic, pleasing solutions – for all situations:

Doorposts: Undercut architraves and the doorpost with a handsaw as far as the height of the new floor and chisel out what is needed – making sure you chisel out enough for the floor to hide its edge, and still have room to expand.

Fireplace: Leave an expansion gap around. When the floor ends lower, pin down a flat solid beading on the floor – covering the gap in a neat and almost flush-way. When your floor ends higher, use a so-called "end-threshold" to finish it off. This will give you the needed expansion gap as a neat, very small, "step" from floor to fire-place.

Stair: If the stair carpet isn't thick enough to cover the gap (most professional carpet fitters will "double-back" the carpet at the bottom of the stair, giving you twice the thickness of the carpet), you can either install a flat beading on the floor, or use mastic filler (curved stairs come to mind). In a few cases you could fill the gap with a flexible cork strip – as long as you can reach the strip to lift it out when the floor threatens to expand!

So remember... as we said before - Leave gaps everywhere – we mere mortals cannot change the laws of physics!

Don't use Cork Strips to Fill your Expansion Gaps!

Some issues keep recurring - cork strips among them.

Two examples of the questions we keep receiving on this subject:

"I realise the importance of leaving an expansion gap around a wooden floor (oak parquet in my case), but can you tell me why we are told to insert cork strips around the edge? Surely the cork is only taking up valuable expansion room. Is it ok to just leave a 10mm gap all around?"

"What a brilliant site for a self builder/renovator/mad diyerect like me. Lots of useful info. Am thinking of installing solid oak 140mm x 18mm t&g plank flooring in a 7m x 2.5m extension we have built around four months ago. My question to you is the only query left that I could not find an answer to and that is: Should I fill the expansion gap with cork as recommended by a variety of manufacturers in their instructions or not and if not why not?"

This is our (recurring) answer on this subject:

"Thank you for your question. We are trying so hard to tell everyone exactly that: **DO NOT use cork strips to fill the expansion gap.**
These were used many, many, years ago to divide design parquet pattern and the block border and somehow ended up in the expansion gap. So, you are absolutely right. Leave your expansion gap "empty" to cater for any natural seasonal movement of your wood floor."

The reply from one:
"Many thanks, it's nice to be right for once!"

Of course he's right; we still don't understand how the old-fashion cork divider strip ended up as recommendation - even by manufacturers! - to fill your expansion gaps with.

Keeping your Wits about Widths!

[Extra info available online - www.woodmanual.co.uk]

This article came to be after a phone call we received from a devastated DIY-er:

"I followed your rules about the gaps, but things have still gone wrong!"

When you need to determine the size of the expansion gap that you have to keep around the whole perimeter of the floor, there are a few "rules of thumb". Especially with Solid Oak flooring, you need 3 - 4 mm gap per meter width of the room. Why? Because that is how much per meter wide Solid Oak can expand during the seasonal changes in air humidity.

It does sound like a simple and easy to follow "rule". That's until we received a phone call last week from a desperate DIY-er. He had kept himself to the rule, his room was 4 meters wide and had kept an expansion gaps all around of 18mm, but the Solid Oak boards (secretly nailed directly on to joists) had started to lift up in two areas. What could be the reason for this? He had checked for leaks and hadn't found anything suspicious.

When we asked some further questions, it turned out that indeed his room was only 4 meter wide, but the joists run parallel to the *long* wall - **a massive 21 meter long wall** (spread over 3 connecting "rooms"). This meant that the new Solid Oak floorboards run row next to row next to row (perpendicular to the direction of the joists), creating in fact **a 21 meter wide area of flooring!**

In this case the length of the room had effectively turned into the width of the room, and another set of "Rules of Thumb" should have been followed:

Never install Solid Oak floorboards in a room wider than 6 meters without adding extra expansion gaps (by way of installing thresholds or flat dividers in the most logical places. For instance, where two rooms have been knocked into one and still have "pillars" or small parts of the old wall).

So, keep your wits about widths, and realise that with installing wooden floors the actual width of the room sometimes has to be measured along the length of the room. It all depends on how you are installing your floorboards: lengthways or widthways!

On those occasions where you install parallel to the shortest wall, the "width" of your floor is the total length of the longest wall! Therefore, in a room measuring 6m x 3m, where the boards are installed parallel to the shortest wall (the 3m wall), you calculate the expansion gap based on the 6 meter width - i.e. leave a gap of at least 24mm, not 12mm for Solid Oak floors.

Glueing, Nailing, Floating - What's What and When to Use

Question:
Hi, really good information on your site... We plan to put a solid wood floor (140mm wide oak planks) onto a concrete floor. House is 8 years old. Planning to do 3 adjoining rooms total of 42 m square. We've been given different advice - some fitters say glue straight to concrete, some say use underlay and glue planks together. Could you give us any advice on this, any help much appreciated.

Answer:
Both methods are suitable. Glueing the solid floor down depends on the condition and quality of the concrete underfloor (the "weakest link"). We ourselves prefer the floating method (when the room isn't wider than 5 meters), installing a combi-underlayment and glueing (with PVAC wood-glue) all Tongues and Grooves. Leave sufficient expansion gaps around the perimeter of the floor which ever method you use. Hope this helps

What's the difference between glueing, secret nailing, and floating? And how does the width of the board affect the method you use?

Methods

- Glueing = Fully bonding the wood to the sub floor.
- Secret Nailing = Nailing, at a 30 - 45 degree angle, the floorboards to batten (at least 5cm thick) or joist.
- Floating = Installing underlayment first on a sub floor, then installing floorboard to "float" on the underlayment, and glueing the tongue and grooves.

Glueing:
This is mostly used with design parquet floors and strip floorboards (narrow boards up to 100mm), or when you have many small lengths of wider boards. Most manufacturers recommend glueing down all floor types when UFH (Underfloor Heating) is involved, to prevent air-pockets.

Narrow floorboards (up to 100mm), and also wood floors which have wider boards but many short lengths (shorter than 50cm), should be glued instead of installed floating. This is because these types of floors will have many joints, each acting as a hinge, meaning that if your floor was installed floating it would be rather unstable and prone to movement. Bonding these boards fully to the underfloor will give it more stability.

Alternatively you can use self-adhesive underlayment (like the original Elastilon), if you want or need extra sound-insulation, or if full bonding is not possible (due to quality of concrete/screed, or when you have modern chipboard with a moist repellent finish).

Secret Nailing:
Used when installing directly onto joists or existing floorboards, or sometimes on a sub floor of thick enough plywood (but remember never to nail on chipboard, as it will split). When you opt for nailing, don't install underlayment between subfloor and the new floor. This will be compressed by the nails and lose its insulating effect.

Floating:
Most solid and wood-engineered boards can be installed floating.
Note for solid: The width of the board should be wider than 100mm, or the width of the room should not exceed 5 - 6 meters - otherwise it is best to glue solid floorboards.
Note for all floor types: Remember what we explained previously about using too many short lengths. If this is the case you had better not install your floor using the floating method, but choose to either fully glue down or use Elastilon self-adhesive underlayment.

The Guide will be based mostly on the "Floating Installation" Method

In most situations this method is the most simple and practical for the majority of DIY-ers.

Separate sections contain tips and advice for the other methods but do read the "floating" section because many tips and tricks of the trade explained there can be used with all installation methods.

The Ongoing Battle of the Floor Installation Methods: Which is Best?

Like "Which is the best finish type for a wooden floor?", this is a question that 'pops-up' frequently in our inbox.

Battle

Why does one professional (or camp of professionals even) say:

"NEVER try to float a tongue and groove glued solid plank floor. Whether you use slip membranes, etc., and gaps at edges, there is a good chance it will eventually split in a zig-zag fashion following the line of least resistance of a board or joint. Stresses within the floor do this, and it makes no difference that the whole thing can move. Apparently called "rafting."

Whilst the other professional (or again, a whole camp of professionals) says: "No problem!"

One of our DIY-clients hopes the following:

"I have 4 months to wait for concrete to dry, so hopefully will they have this sorted out by then!"

Sorted?

Sorted? We're afraid not - this is one of those "Battles of the Methods" where one camp will always follow one method - through own personal experiences with the method that gives them and their clients the least problems, and the way they have been taught by their mentors during their apprenticeship - and the other camp will keep following their preferred alternative method of installing solid floorboards.

The best method? Simply, as long as the chosen method is done correctly, any method is fine... depending of course on the circumstances, the product, and the preference of both fitter and client.

The example above on floorboards splitting when using the floating method is mostly down to incorrect glueing of the tongue and grooves. Wood works, and will indeed find the "weakest link" in the whole construction. Tongue & Grooves should be glued completely, not just with drips and drops. (See our own article on "The correct way of glueing Tongue &Grooves").

We have seen wooden floors fully bonded to the underfloor (concrete or sheet material), which come away because the adhesive was applied incorrectly - spread out flat instead of using a notched trowel. We've also seen whole floors "rattle" on their battens, when the battens used were too thin, installed on concrete, and used with the secret nailing (50mm nails) method.

Will there ever be the one method that is followed by all camps? Don't hold your breath. Manufacturers of solid floorboards have their own preferences too, but more and more they give various options in their instructions (fully bonded, floating, secret nailed) as suitable methods of installation, each depending on the specific circumstances in your home.

Again, as long as your situation allows it, any method is fine ONLY when done the correct way.

Installing using the "Floating" method

Glueing Tongue & Groove Boards the Correct Way

Question:
I've had a so called 'professional' partially lay my timberjack solid rustic oak flooring before walking out on me. The floorboards are random lengths from 400-1800mm, width 140mm with normal T&G. He's put the boards on a foam underlay covering the concrete floor but he has not glued the wood together. Is that correct?

Answer
Your fitter should have glued all T&G's properly (from top to bottom in the groove). You now have the risk that when the floor shrinks, gaps will appear everywhere between the joints.

There seems to be some strange advice around on how to glue Tongue & Groove boards, when using the "floating installation" method.

What Not To Do

Recently we have seen how wrongly applying the PVAC wood glue can cause problems - in the short and long run. Where the adhesive was applied on the underlayment in front of the already installed row of boards, with the idea that installing the next row would "scoop up" enough glue to bond the boards together.

A) It doesn't work, and some parts of the Tongue & Groove will not have enough adhesive, thus creating a "weak" link.

B) Residue glue will be left on the underlayment, bonding part of the boards to the underlayment, which can cause an obstruction when the wood expands or shrinks.

Another "bright idea" is to apply drops of adhesive instead of a whole length. Again, this will cause many weak links in the construction of your floor.

With the floating method **ALL Tongue & Grooves have to be glued completely and of every board.** There's no two ways about it, and no "saving" money in the short run. And really, are bottles of PVAC wood glue so expensive compared with the costs and time of having to re-install the floor (and probably replacing many damaged boards where the tongues and grooves have broken off) because of this "drip and drop" method?

The Correct Way

So, what is the best method?

A PVAC wood glue bottle comes with an 'adjustable' nozzle. Depending on the size of the groove (narrow, medium or wide) you just select where to cut off the nozzle. Remember: you can always go "bigger", but you can never stick it back on - so better too little than too much!
Hold the board you're about to install in your hand, and apply the adhesive in the bottom part of the groove, for the whole length of the groove. You'll find your own "best practice", but we normally start at the lowest end of the groove and work our way up. Do the same with the short end groove.

When installing the glued board, the sliding movement will spread the adhesive "around" the tongue of the board on the row already installed. This is especially important with Wood-Engineered flooring, where the tongue is made of cross-layered wood (pine) which has a more open structure. Not enough adhesive on this open structure could create a weak link.

Any seepage out of the adhesive on the top of the board should be removed with a damp cloth straight away.

As with other installation methods... **keep it simple and keep it clean for the best results.**

Installing a Floating Wood Floor: Keep it Simple
[Extra info available online - www.woodmanual.co.uk]

Installation of solid or wood-engineered floors, with standard Tongue and Groove construction, using the "floating" method is the most often used method by DIY-ers because it involves no extra special materials like heavy tubs of adhesive, big nails or nail-guns. It can be used in 9 out of 10 situations without any problems.

It isn't rocket science. It's more a case of common sense, patience, buying the right quality and using the correct materials.

And of course you have to take all the correct preparations before you start the actual installation.

Recap of Preparations:

Some things are so obvious; we won't go into them in detail here. Things like buying wood that is suitable to be installed as floor, and dry enough (meaning: timber wood with 15% moisture or more isn't suitable), that the room is wind and weather proof, and all wet decoration work is finished, etc.

Correct Materials and Correct Preparations:
Quality products might be a little dearer; but in the end it will save you time, aggravation, and possibly even regret (not to mention money!).

Make sure you have **one type of underfloor,** and that the underfloor is ready (dry, level, existing floor-coverings have been removed with plenty of time to make good any defects or unevenness.

Buy the **correct underlayment** suitable for your type of underfloor.

Have **ALL the materials in house** before you start. Make a list of everything you need at least one week beforehand, and make sure it can be delivered or collected on time (because some materials just run out of stock... you'll know Murphy's Law).

Make sure **all the tools you need are in the house**, all are working, sharp and safe. If you have to hire specific tools, place a reservation on them with the hire company, so you're not going to be disappointed on the vital day.

Store the wood in the same area you plan to lay it (or in an area that has the same 'climate conditions'. Garages are a definite No No!
It's 2 – 4 days for wood-engineered floors.

And 2 - 3 weeks for solid floors (if you know where it has been stored before, otherwise leave it longer).

This is the MINIMUM time to store it before you start the installation. Leave the wood in the packs, if it is wrapped in packaging material, and according to manufacturer's instructions. Some do differ, most not.

Clear all furniture out of the room beforehand. The dust from sawing will get into everything!

Remove – if needed – skirting boards. Mark them when you do, so that you know which one to place back where, and avoid mix-ups and extra cutting work when placing them back.

Preparations on the Day

Ban Little Children from the Room! (Along with cats, dogs and assorted other pets!). It may also be worth banning any "helpful" relatives and neighbours, who are there only to keep asking "Have you nearly finished?"

Make a final check that all materials and tools are there.

Materials: Wood (fairly obviously), underlayment, pvac-wood glue, spacers, beading or scotia, radiator-pipe-covers, thresholds, plenty of cloths (to remove excess glue as soon as you notice), and felt pads (for use underneath furniture). Spacers are used to set out your expansion gaps. For wood-engineered floors this should be a minimum of 10mm all around, for solid floors see the rule of thumbs in the chapter "Solid floors - what to note". Remember - NEVER EVER fill your expansion gap with cork or anything else!

Tools: Hand saw or jig-saw, tape-measure, square, Stanley knife, pencils (at least three, they disappear into thin air), knocking block and jemmy bar (both can be part of any DIY installation kit you buy - but are not always of the best quality), hammer, heavy duty bin bags, work bench (tool box can also be fine also as bench, but watch you don't saw into it!).

If needed, **remove doors** and undercut architrave and/or doorposts (chisel out the last bit).

Open two packs of wood, and check for any **damage** to the surfaces, tongue and groove, or click-system. If you find any, and on more boards, re-pack as best as possible and return every pack straight back to your supplier for new material, or re-fund. In no circumstances open more packs to check for damage, as this might render your guarantee useless.

Check if the boards are **straight** by laying them with the groove side on the (level) underfloor. Also check for bowing – cupping. Slight bowing (middle doesn't touch the ground) of long boards is normal. Extreme cupping - the ends stand up and leave a gap of over 5cm if turned upside down (i.e. top surface faces floor) is not.

If everything is OK, and in the wood-type, grade and finish you selected, mix the two packs to get a natural look and colour/shade mixture (all boards differ in colour and characteristics). During the work, **keep checking** for surface damages before you install a board. Once down and between other boards, it's a pain to remove it. (Murphy's Law: it will always end up in the middle of the room where you would notice it most).

Do read the fitting instructions (if any) the manufacturer supplied with the floor. Some might differ on certain points, and not following their instructions could render your guarantee worthless. When in doubt, call your supplier.

The Basic Installation Tips

These tips are based on laying a wooden floor in a normal straight forward rectangular room, without any obstacles or problems, and under normal circumstances. We know that other shaped rooms will differ, but the practice and use of common sense is the same.

Start at the wall that has the fewest doors, bay windows, fireplaces, alcoves or recesses and seems straight.

Lay the first row of underlayment parallel to the chosen wall from one end of the room to the other. When using DPM or Combi-underlayment, move the row at least 3 - 5 cm up the walls. Make sure that you place the Combi-underlayment in such way that the overlapping DPM strip is on the room side, not the wall side.

Place the first board on top of the underlayment in a corner where both grooves (long side and short side) face the walls of that corner (some instructions state you have to start in a specific corner, so use common practical sense).

Glue the groove on the short side of the next board (at the bottom of the groove to avoid glue splurting out above) and connect board one and two, making sure that there is no gap between the joint. A gap at one end of the joint indicates your boards aren't connected straight. Don't worry about spacers just now.

Install the complete first row this way (use the knocking block if needed). Keep checking for gaps between the joints.

The last board might need to be cut. If this cut off is longer than 300mm (1 foot), use this as the first board in the next row. It will still have its tongue to connect with the groove of the next full board.

Avoid Fixed Pattern of Joints: A Useful Trick of the Trade

In rectangular rooms and with fixed length boards you run the risk of creating a fixed patterns of joints.

Every time you start a row with a new board, your cut-off piece from the last board in that row will have the same length as the pieces you started earlier rows with, creating this best-avoided fixed pattern.

See the (online) image below for an example of this fixed pattern - looking like brickwork.

Creating a pattern like this will also increase your amount of saw-waste. We had a (builder) client once who came back twice (!) for more materials. Had he measured the rooms incorrectly we asked? No, he'd checked that more than once, he just kept running out of materials. When we delivered the extra materials we realised they'd started in one rectangular room with a fixed pattern to save time. Other rooms had other dimensions but they still continued the same pattern - and now needed to cut off material from each end board to keep the pattern. Being a large job, in the end it costs them over 20 sq m extra wood.

If they had started the first room with a deliberate staggered pattern, the normal amount of saw-waste would have been enough to see them through without the need to order extra materials.

Simple solution: If the cut off is long enough, say 600mm cut off 200mm so you're left with a starter piece of 400mm (make sure you still have the tongue!) or cut off a bit of a full board (again, make sure you still are left with the tongue!). This way even in a rectangular room with boards of a fixed length you are able to stagger the boards randomly.

Ensure the First Row is a Straight Row, No Matter how Bendy your Wall is.

Make sure all the joints of row 1 fit tightly and are straight.

Straight joints means all individual boards are connected to each other without any gaps in the joints. It could be that the first row isn't "straight" following your wall, but that is in this instance of no consequence.

Next, move your row slightly away from the wall - enough to place your spacers. Use thicker and thinner ones depending on the "quality" of your wall and skirting boards, then move row one back against the spacers. Once this is done, check all the joints again.

Making sure your first row is straight is the most important step of the installation.

If needed use extra thin material behind some of the spacers to ensure the first row is straight.

The Main Part of the Room

Install the rest of the room, installing subsequent rows of underlayment as you go. With Combi-underlayment make sure the overlapping self-adhesive strip fits correctly underneath the next row of underlayment.

Glue both long side and short side grooves of all boards, before slotting them in place. Make sure to glue the whole of the groove length, not just drops here and there. (Do read the article: How to glue Tongue & Groove boards correctly.)

Remove any excess adhesive with a damp cloth as soon as possible. When needed use the knocking block and/or installation bar for a tight fit and keep checking those joints. Place spacers at the beginning and the end of some of the rows, to keep your expansion gap the same everywhere.

Don't walk over the boards you've just installed.

Take a well-deserved coffee or tea break after you installed row four, so the glue gets time to bond. Then carry on with the rest of the floor.

Tackling the Last Row: A Trick of the Trade

Don't worry, it's not a nightmare (not with standard Tongue & Groove boards anyway), but common sense and patience will help get you there.
All you need is two new boards and some spacers (you could use cut-offs from your own floor as spacers here - they are not there to stay) - See also the online image.

Place the spacers against the wall or skirting board (you might need some assistance here to help you keep the spacers upright).
New board 1 - You place exactly over the last board installed (so the tongue faces the wall).

New Board 2 - (Again with the tongue facing the wall) You place over new board 1 and you slide board 2 to the spacers.

With a pencil you **trace the edge of board 2 on board 1** - this (overlapped by board 2) will be the exact piece you need to cut off.

You will end up with a cut board that fits properly, AND you have created the needed expansion gap, all in one go. Glue the groove of the board, and install the last row board by board.

Doorways!

Another trick of the trade here. How to install a board neatly in doorways (located parallel the direction of the boards) and still leave a wide enough expansion gap.

Before you started the installation you should have undercut every door post in the room (far enough for the needed expansion gap). In most cases the board that ends in the doorway will also continue along the wall at both sides of the door, so the board needs to be cut in two places to cater for this. Once you've made your measurements and cut off the two bits (leaving a wide bit on the board where it goes in the doorway) you have to install the board: sliding it underneath the doorposts for a neat finish AND connecting it with the row already installed.

Remember those sliding puzzles, movable slides in a fixed frame with one little empty space? That's the principle of what we're going to do here too.

The last complete board in front of the door opening goes in AFTER the "cut to size board" has received its glue in the groove and is slided as far as possible underneath the doorpost. Next, glue the groove of the board not yet installed and install this. Then slide back the "cut-to-size" board so it connects with the other board and at the same time leaves (again) sufficient expansion room underneath the doorpost.
(One of the reasons you have to undercut your doorposts far enough, otherwise this will not work.)

Tip: try out if it all fits without glueing the two involved boards first, you might need to re-do your "cut-to-size" board when sliding it back reveals a gap between board and doorpost.

The Finishing Touches

Remove all packaging and leftover boards etc from the room. Vacuum clean the room (or use a soft broom) to remove all the sawdust and little pieces of wood, before they can damage the floor when walked on.

Remove spacers, and install scotia, beading or skirting boards in place. Look out for lost or dropped nails and pins - undetected they can damage your floor before you've even finished, if they are trodden on.
Remove everything from the room (tools, etc), and vacuum clean again. Wait 2 - 3 hours before placing furniture back, to give the glue time to bond. Walking and moving furniture around might open any boards and create gaps (Murphy's law: normally in the middle of the room).

Stick felt pads underneath legs of chairs and table to prevent scratches.

As we mentioned before: these are **BASIC tips:** Rooms and circumstances may vary. In most other situations the best tip is to think ahead, use common sense and patience.

Installing using the "Glue Down" method
Glueing Basics
[Extra info available online - www.woodmanual.co.uk]

Question:
Hi I am going to be laying a solid wood floor on concrete that is very old - 40 yrs min i think. I have a few questions: I want to face fix and glue onto 12mm ply. what is the best glue to use? I will be laying the air bubble and foil insulation which is 4mm thick under the ply. Do I need to lay acoustic underlay on top of the ply? I hope to use 180mm sawn oak boards - planks basically with no t&g. Do I need to do anything special with this type of wood ? What is the difference between this wood and t&g. Is the t&g option better ? Thanks very much for your help.

Answer:
If you glue down, you can't use another underlayment between ply and boards. The best adhesive to use would be a flexible adhesive (like Mapei P990). Make sure the Oak boards are dried to floor standard (moisture content in the wood between 9 - 11%), and can acclimatise in the room you plan to have them installed in. The difference between your boards and T&G boards is that T&G's can be installed floating, secretly nailed or fully glued down. Boards without T&G should be glued and pinned down (as you plan to do).

Glueing down (or fully bonding) a wood floor is also a frequently used way of installation, and in certain situations you don't have any other choice than to use this method. Below we'll show you how, and advise on using this method for floor boards. Although you also install herringbone blocks and other design parquet using the fully bonded method, it is quite a different subject - and will be covered in our next manual.

Underfloor or Subfloor

In the preparation section we've already covered how to get your underfloor ready, so we shouldn't need to go into much detail again here. We do want to stress that, especially with this method, you will get the best results when your underfloor is sound, solid, dry, level and in good condition. With the floating installation you could get away with some small defects in the underfloor, but you will regret not making adequate preparations here. If needed, you have to install a suitable subfloor on top of your crumbled concrete, damaged existing floorboards, and especially modern chipboard with its moist repellent surface layer - on to which no current adhesive will hold! So, if needed, revisit the preparation section of this manual to make sure you start the installation of your new floor boards in the best possible way.

Correct Materials

For floorboards you need to use a flexible adhesive, not an adhesive that is only suitable for wood blocks or mosaic. Flexible here means that it will hold its bond between underfloor and top floor longer when the wood floor shrinks or expands during normal seasonal changes in humidity. In other words, it doesn't prevent the wood floor from behaving in its natural way! (None of the installation methods will prevent natural movement, but any properly executed installation method will prevent minor and major problems).

See the list of recommended products for brand names and usages.

One other important tool you need to have is a correctly notched trowel to create the right ridges in the adhesive. Spreading out the adhesive, and just plonking down the board on it, will not give the correct bonding you're after. The adhesive would then just be a thin layer between underfloor and wood floor, having no "grip" at all.

As you will see in the drawing online in the extras, with a notched trowel (A) the adhesive (B) is spread in ridges on the underfloor (C), thus ensuring that every board connects with the adhesive on as large a surface area as possible (at least 85% of your board should connect with the adhesive).

You can imagine that when a board has a little flex of its own, creating ridges instead of a flat surface of adhesive will give you a much better chance of establishing this minimum percentage of contact. On the other hand, don't consider your adhesive as a filler for dips in your underfloor. It can tackle minor dips, but don't rely on it to make good every dip or damaged area of your underfloor because it won't.

Directions

With the notched trowel, spread the adhesive (B) perpendicular to the direction of your floorboards (D) to decrease the movement of the flexible adhesive during normal circumstances. (Note: image online in the extras is to show correct way of applying glue only, "floorboards" there are in fact wood blocks, hence the recurring pattern).
Wood works itself width-ways, and hardly at all length-ways, so if you install your board in the same direction as the ridges the combination of flexibility and normal movement could create a "sliding" effect. Applying the adhesive as shown above will prevent this, but will still give your boards the bonding it needs. It will also combine the flexibility to keep its bonding when seasonal shrinkage or expansion occurs.

You do not need to glue the tongue and groove's of the boards, bonding your floorboards with the flexible adhesive on the underfloor is sufficient.

Other Practices

Follow the tips and advice from the installation basics, and the floating installation method, to install your floor. Besides the adhesive and notched trowel versus underlayment and PVAC wood glue for the tongue and grooves, there are no real differences in the two methods.

When you have finished your installation, leave the floor to settle for 8 - 10 hours before placing any furniture back. This will allow the adhesive to bond fully.

Fact Sheet - Wood and Underfloor Heating Systems

Question:
I have a bungalow with suspended wooden floors and am considering installing a wet Underfloor heating over the floor boards.
On top of the ufh I would like a wooden floor. Which would be best, engineered board or solid wood?

Answer:
Definitely wood-engineered. The construction of the wood-engineered makes it much more stable in this situation.
Our Duoplank Oak range is guaranteed on underfloor heating, but most other wood-engineered boards are suitable too.

Duoplank flooring has proven to be among the most stable wooden floor products on the market. Four wood species have been tested by a Dutch laboratory, TNO. The RC Value for oak is 0,12. You can contact the supplier of the heating system to check if the effect for your system is ok.

Many other wood-engineered products are highly suitable too, such as Wood You Like's Triplank range. The cross-layered backing gives it more stability, and is not prone to shrink as much as solid boards can when installed almost directly onto a heat source. We do recommend you check if the product you buy is suitable, and suggest you follow the recommendation of the manufacturer on preparation/installation instructions.

General Guidelines

To obtain the best performance of your floor in the long term, it's important to follow these guidelines. As there is no reliable way of recording or monitoring the heating-systems settings and room conditions over time, it would be impossible to prove or disprove whether all the guidelines have been followed. Therefore we can not give a guarantee.

In practice, any floor is almost certain to shrink when used with an underfloor heating system, and there will be some movement of the floor. This is due to the relatively high moisture content. After a month's use with an under-floor heating system, the level of the moisture in the wood drops, and this loss of moisture manifests itself as shrinkage. If the moisture loss is severe, there can also be a breakdown in the cellular structure of the wood that leads to splits in the wear-layer (this can happen with Jatoba and Maple for example).

Some species are more suitable for use with an under-floor heating system than others. The following species in the Duoplank range have been tested and proven to be stable:
- European Oak
- Merbau
- Walnut
- Iroko

Steps to Take

If you install a wood-engineered floor on a under floor heated sub floor, there are **some conditions you should respect:**

- Tubes should be located a minimum of 3cm below the surface of the screed.
- The screed must dry naturally to below 1,8% moisture content (anhydrite: 0,3%). Do not turn the under-floor heating on before the correct moisture level is achieved.
- The maximum temperature of the surface of the screed should be 28°C, and steady.
- Relative atmospheric humidity should be maintained between 50-65%, adjust by ventilating, or using a humidifier.
- Make sure the boards can acclimatise in the area for 3 to 7 days before installation. Keep air temperature between 10°C and 20°C, and relative atmospheric humidity between 50-65%.
- Leave the board in the shrink-wrapped foil until the installation.
- The use of standard, micro bevelled planks will minimise the visual impact of shrinkage. A square edge board will show up the shrinkage much more through slight gapping.

Before installation:
- Heat up the water of the system to 20°C.
- Raise the temperature every day by 5°C until a maximum of 45°C.
- Maintain this temperature for 5 days.
- In the following days, lower the temperature by 5°C every day, until you reached the temperature of 20°C again.
- Then turn off the system.

Installation of the wood-engineered floor:
- A PU-based adhesive, such as Sika T54, Mapei P990, or similar should be used, and will act as both adhesive, moisture barrier, and thermal conductor.
- Wood should be sealed as soon as possible after laying. Oiled floors should be fed and maintained more often than conventional, non under-floor heated floors.

After installation of the wood-engineered floor:
- After fitting, the floor should be allowed to cure for 7 days before the heating is turned on.
- The heating should initially be turned on at the ambient temperature.
- It should then be raised by no more than 1°C per day until the required temperature is reached.
- The room temperature should be maintained between 20°-23°C.
- The heating system should be run in strict accordance with the manufacters' instructions.
- Beware of leaving solid furniture and/or heavy rugs in one position for any length of time. If the floor is "capped" in this way, this will lead to cupping and gapping, from which the floor may not be able to recover.

Glueing - Case-study: Duoplank on Underfloor Heating

[Extra info available online - www.woodmanual.co.uk]

(Guest article by John and Julie - West Berkshire)

The Situation

"As self-builders, we are very involved in specifying the materials used in our house. We wanted the look and feel of real oak planks, but without too many of the difficulties associated with the shrinkage of natural oak. We quickly identified the Duoplank product through its UK distributor, Wood-You-Like, in Kent. This is an Engineered Board made with a wide top solid layer of natural oak, and a high-quality birch ply substrate, which was critical to us because we were installing on concrete with UFH embedded in the floor.

We visited the showroom near Ashford and received plenty of good advice from the company, and felt we were dealing with people who actually installed the product, as well as supplying it.

The Selection

From the wide range of oak qualities available, we selected the 'Rustic' range as being closest to the effect we sought to create in our new-build - a Georgian-style farmhouse of brick and tile exterior.

The Installation

Installing the product was easier than we expected, with the longest task being the selecting and cutting of the planks. As we tackled each room, we initially placed them in position 'dry' on the floor to check for colour-match and fit. The planks slot together using a tongue-and-groove formation. The Duoplank manufacturer had taken care to chamfer the bottom edges of the planking, avoiding any chance of surplus glue seeping into the tongue-and-grooves. We used a chop-saw to cut each edging plank to length. This made light work of the cutting task, even though the engineered product seemed as dense as working with solid oak. We glued the rows of board to the floor, three or four at a time.

Wood-You-Like had given us a clear instructions (included in Guide) on how to pre-condition the boards, and the temperature of the floor during the installation. This ensures that the boards have a normal amount of humidity on installation. Unlike a conventionally heated house, when using UFH the wood flooring shrinks slightly in the winter whilst heat is drawn up through the floor.

Expansion gaps and tools

Wood-You-Like advised us on the size of the gap to leave around the wall edges - 15mm in our case - and we used chipboard spacers to maintain this gap, and hold the edges firm whilst we glued and fitted each successive row. We found a notched trowel to be best tool for spreading the glue evenly. It was important for us to eliminate air gaps under the boards to maximise heat transfer from the screed into the wood. We managed this by spreading the glue 'notches' at 90 degrees to the board lengths, which enables one to see better where the boards are not fully seated, as glue oozes out slightly at the working edge. We used bricks as a temporary method of holding down any 'high' areas of board during setting. This task certainly showed up minor inadequacies in the flatness of the screed sub floor! Fitting the 25mm wide skirting board around the rooms to cover this gap has completed the finished appearance.

The Result

The glue sets in 24 hours, and we followed the detailed instructions for gradually applying heat into the flooring to slowly dry out the wood. During our first winter heating season this has opened up a 1mm gap at many of the board long edges - or about 0.05% total shrinkage compared to the summer state, when we expect the gap to close up again. We are more than happy with this result over UFH, and our choice of Engineering Board to provide the visual effect that we sought."

Installing using the "Secret Nail" method

Secret Nailing: Installing a Wooden Floor on Battens... Is it Worth the Trouble?

Question:
We are building a house and have solid oak planks which we would like to prepare and lay on a cement floor. We only have 4 cm space to lay the floor. Should we glue down battens, 2cm high, and then nail the planks to the battens?

Answer
Why install battens on a presumably new concrete floor? If this is sound, level, and dry, installing battens is in our opinion a waste of money, materials and effort. Any way, 2cm (20mm) high battens will not be high enough to nail into. A good alternative would be to install your wood floor using the floating method, using a combi-underlayment that contains a DPM and sound-insulation. This will all keep within the 4cm space you have for the floor.

One question regularly asked about installing wooden flooring concerns the secret nailing method, when there is a concrete underfloor involved. "The fitter wants to use battens to install the floor, what materials do you advise?" or "We have a concrete floor, do we need to install battens to install the solid floorboards?"

Battens on Concrete - a Choice?

In 9 out of the 10 situations, installing battens on to a perfectly sound concrete floor isn't needed. It only costs extra for materials, adds work, and loses room height. Most times a new wood floor can be installed directly onto the concrete using the floating or fully glueing method. We're still not sure why some fitters insist on the nailing method, as in most situations it's a waste of material (money) and effort.

If, however, you do need to cover up bad quality/crumbled concrete/screed, plan to hide a tremendous amount of cabling between the concrete and the wood floor, or your underfloor heating system is placed in between battens, then you can install battens as long as you follow some simple rules:

Rules of Thumb

The battens should be at least 50mm high, and 50mm wide but if possible 75mm wide.
The reason: the nails used to secret nail the floorboard onto the battens should be at least 50 - 60mm long, and if you use lower battens there is a high risk the nail will hit the concrete before it firmly holds down the board. The extra width of the battens gives every board sufficient room to "rest" on - i.e. extra stability.

Battens should be installed not further apart than 35 - 40cm, and preferably **screwed down** (countersunk, or you can use hammer fixings) every 25 cm, or **glued down** with flexible adhesive.

The floorboards need to be load-bearing - at least 18mm thick - and long enough to connect with at least 3 battens. If your floorboards have tongue and groove's on all 4 sides you don't need to end every board on a batten, as long as you follow the "3 batten" rule.

T-nails with ribbed (serrated) teeth should be between 50 - 60mm long, and nailed in a 30 - 40 degree angle just behind the Tongue of the board. The best tool to use is a manual Portanailer or an airgun - with a special foot attachment.

Underlayment - if needed - should be installed between the battens, not on the battens. The force and the angle of the nail will compress the underlayment, which makes the sound-insulation properties of the underlayment almost useless.

Secret Nailing on Existing Floorboards - Plywood
[Extra info available online - www.woodmanual.co.uk]

Question:
Hi, Silly question but I've been reading loads about how to install a wooden floor onto an existing wooden floor and I'm probably going to try the secret nailing method. (Here comes the silly question)...Do I have to nail all the floorboards? I only ask because I was wondering, how will the floor be able to expand and contract if it's nailed to the floor underneath?? Sorry if this sounds really daft but just want to clarify the situation. Many thanks

Answer:
First of all, silly questions don't exist (only silly answers ;-)) Yes, you do have to nail all boards (every 40 - 50 cm but at least two nails per board) otherwise when the floor expands or shrinks the 'loose' boards can buckle or cup more easily. Wood expands/shrinks due to changes in air-humidity during the various seasons, no matter what method you use for installation. The nails will hold them in place better to prevent gaps (when shrinking) or cupping (when expanding). Hope this clarifies it for you

Some wood floor manufacturers insist you install their product using the secret nail method. And some floor fitters deem this the only proper way of installing a solid wood floor. As we've said many times before: wood works, no matter which installation method you select. Nailing your floorboards will not stop the natural movement of the boards during the seasonal changes in humidity, it can only reduce the effect on gaps and/or cupping (when installed properly and with the right preparations taken in account).

Floorboards or Plywood as "Underfloor"

The best results - again - will be achieved when your underfloor is sound, level and in overall good nick. With existing floorboards, make sure they are still securely fixed to the joists, and if needed replace those parts you doubt the quality or longevity of. Walk over your existing floor to detect any loose connections (creaking), and if needed fix those boards down more securely.

Plywood on concrete or chipboard: The nail you are using to fix the new floorboards to the subfloor should be 50 - 60mm long, so you have to make sure the "subfloor" of plywood is thick enough for the nail to get a good grip. 6 - 12mm won't do this, 18mm perhaps will (on chipboard). You can of course opt to install thick enough battens first, then plywood (18mm because it needs to be load-bearing). If you opt for this solution, the total thickness of plywood (at least 18mm) and batten should be at least 50mm.

Direction

When your underfloor consists of the existing floorboards it is highly recommended to install your new boards at a 90 degree angle (perpendicular) to the direction of the existing boards, to prevent a see-saw effect from cupped old boards. If that's not possible, or it would not look aesthetically right, you'll need to board over your existing floorboards first with 6 or 12mm plywood, (depending on the levelness of the existing boards). The plywood has to be (counter) screwed or stapled every 25 cm, and between the plywood sheets you have to leave a small gap ("credit card thickness") to allow movement of the ply itself during the seasons. Don't forget to leave a 10mm gap around the perimeter of the plywood subfloor!

The Difference in Installation Steps Compared with Floating or Glueing.

Only minor differences:
The first row always starts with the groove towards the wall - no matter the instructions of the manufacturer (if these differ, you should start to worry about the quality of the product or at least the translation of the instructions!).

The last row you can nail will be determined by the width of your board - you do need to have room to place the nailer and if applicable manoeuvre the mallet/hammer.
If this is no longer possible, glue all tongue and grooves of the remaining rows in the correct way, and make sure the last row is "fixed" underneath the skirting boards - or at least underneath a doorpost.

Angle and Nails

Use T-nails with ribbed (serrated) teeth, which should be between 50 - 60mm long.
Nail in a 30 - 40 degree angle, just behind the tongue of the board. Best tool to use is a manual Portanailer or an airgun - with special foot attachment set at the correct angle.

Underlayment – none!
The force and the angle of the nail will impress the underlayment, which makes the sound-insulation properties the underlayment has almost useless. If you installed plywood over battens, and you do need extra insulation, it should be installed between the battens, not between plywood and wood floor.

Secret Nailing: Installing a Wooden Floor on Joists

Question:
As someone who is considering a wooden floor, planning on doing it themself, and trying to get it right first time, I always read your very informative RSS feed. I notice however you often focus your articles toward the modern way of installing flooring: that is tongue and groove, on a solid floor. Being in a listed property, when I replace my flooring it will have to be solid planks (no tongue) and on a suspended floor (ground floor). So my question is, how does this affect preparation and installation? Thanks and regards.

Answer:
Thank you for your comment, and you are right that we focus more on the modern installation ways because 90 out of 100 floors can be (and are) installed on 'modern' underfloors. This doesn't mean other 'old-fashion' ways are forgotten, or not suitable any more. Your own circumstances are a great example of this. Before we can answer your question properly, can we ask how the existing floor is installed? On battens, directly on joists or laying on bare ground (that does happen, we've seen and heard it before).

And the story continued as follows:

Replacing Old Pine Boards

It's a 200-year-old listed mid-terrace cottage. The majority of rooms still have the original boards, which are in a serviceable condition (a great testament to the use of oak in itself!). The room I am looking to work in has a few original boards, but the majority of it is new ply or pine boards, all covered with carpet.

The existing boards are laid directly on joists. The joists have centres of around 400 to 500mm. All boards are nailed to the joists. The underfloor void is about 300 to 400mm high above bare ground. This void is not currently ventilated with air bricks, and while this isn't causing too many problems it is something we are looking to rectify. We are also looking at ways to enable ventilation between the room and the underfloor void.

Being in a listed property, when I replace my flooring it will have to be solid planks and on a suspended floor (ground floor).

So my question is, how does this affect preparation and installation? I'm thinking specifically of underlays (something to protect the wood, not cause condensation, and reduce sound transfer, but remain breathable). Also of fixing methods - I would rather not glue (difficult to take up again) - what are the alternatives?

Finally, I'm also interested in the choice of wood. I have read 18mm thick wood is not sufficient for a suspended floor?

I hope you may have an opportunity to address these questions, and am fairly sure the answers will interest a broad range of people.

Thanks and regards.

Answer (options, tips and issues to be aware of)

Installing directly onto joists above a void (which should indeed have air bricks to insure ventilation - especially for removing excess humidity) asks for floorboards that are at least 18mm thick, though 20 – 21 mm is preferred. Another issue to consider is the space between the joist: 350 - 400 mm is best otherwise the boards may 'flex' too much and could even break or snap.

Normally we would advise solid (or load-bearing Wood-Engineered) floorboards to be installed directly onto the joists by secret nailing in the tongue. If the void underneath is ventilated properly, and doesn't show any signs of moisture, no extra underlayment is needed.

Ventilation causes air movement, which equals draft, but is important to keep your house climate healthy.

The 'modern' construction of the tongue and groove boards allows movement (shrinkage especially) of the boards without feeling the effect of this draft. Filling gaps between 'old-fashion' floorboards is just a very temporary solution, as after a while the filling material will drop in the void because of seasonal movement, and you have to start all over again... and again... and again.

Oak floorboards of 21mm thick **without T&G** can be face-nailed on top of the joists (but note maximum space between joists), as long as every board rests on at least three joists. Because the short sides of the boards don't have connecting tongue and groove's for stability, it's recommended to end every board on a joist.

As mentioned above, non tongue and groove boards can create draft, but we also see another problem. Sourcing proper Oak floorboards suitable for installing as floor. These boards need to be dried to floor specifications, which is between 9 and 11% moisture. Most kiln and dried timber contains 15% moisture.

Solid or load-bearing wood-engineered boards **with Tongue & Groove** can be installed using the secret nailing method. Again, note the maximum space between the joists, and as long as every board connects with at least 3 joists there is no need to end every board on a joist. So make sure you have long enough boards (and be aware of the so-called cheap offers in solid flooring, see our article in this respect).

The tongue and groove construction on all 4 sides of the boards will prevent flexing of the boards **IF** the space between two joists in not wider than 35 - 40 cm.

FINISHING
UNFINISHED FLOORS

Finishing unfinished floors

Most Important Issues and Sanding

Question:
Hi - We've just laid a solid oak floor on the whole of our ground floor and have bought some Blanchon Hard Waxoil to treat it. I applied a coat in the lounge (easy-peasy) but the instructions on the can then say "Polish immediately after applying the product ... to give the wooden floor a uniform finish". However, immediately after applying, the waxoil was still 'wet'. Was I supposed to walk on the waxoil and polish it whilst still 'wet' or wait until it had completely dried and hardened? And if I was supposed to polish it whilst still 'wet', was I actually supposed to do, say, a one meter square section at a time, i.e. applying the waxoil and then immediately polishing, section by section?

In the event I waited for about 20 minutes and then buffed it with a cloth but by then it was very tacky and EXTREMELY hard work - my socks kept sticking to it. Fortunately (I really don't know how) but I seem to have achieved a really good finish but I'm not convinced I've done it right. Therefore before I embark on the hall and dining room I'd be very grateful for your advice.

By the way, yours is a GREAT site - I really wished we'd discovered it before we'd even laid the first plank!!

Answer:
Thank you for your story. In fact polishing should read: buff the floor after applying a thin coat of HardWaxOil to spread it out evenly. Best is to use a buffing machine with a medium coarse pad (brown or beige). If you don't have one, a non-fluffy cloth will do. And indeed, you walk over the freshly applied oil but the buffing will remove any footsteps.

You are right in doing the floor in little sections, applying the HardWaxOil thinly, buffing it out and even spreading it over untreated areas. After you've applied it this way on to the whole floor, let it dry for 8 - 10 hours and apply a second coat the same way. Don't wait longer than 48 hours to apply the second coat though, otherwise you have to lightly sand the floor again.

Hope this helps and good luck with the other rooms.

Always, Always, Always!

When applying any type of finish, READ the instructions on the tin, and follow them! They're there for a very good reason - to give you the best end result.

Sorry, we didn't mean to shout, but lately on various DIY-forums we encounter the same 'problem' being posted. 'After sanding and applying two coats of HardWaxOil, the floor looks patchy'. When we then ask how soon after the first layer the second layer has been applied, most times the answer is 'after 4 - 5 days'.

Never, ever leave it that late between applying the two coats of HardWaxOil. All brands (be it Osmo, Blanchon, or another) specifically write on their instructions 'Apply the second coat within 36 - 48 hours'. Otherwise, the grain-hairs of the wood 'stick-up' and the floor needs a light sanding first.

Read the instructions, no matter what type of finish you plan to apply, and if you're still in doubt call for advice. Every proper supplier has either a company sticker with contact details on the tin, or the manufacturers help-line is printed on it.

Last Sanding Round

It is highly recommended to sand an unfinished floor after it has been installed. Not only to create a smooth surface when the boards feel rough, but also to remove greasy fingerprints and excess - spilled - glue. If you do not remove these they will definitely affect the appearance of the final finish.

If there are many height differences start with grit 80, if the floor feels smooth use 120. For **oil finishes**: The maximum grit to use in last sanding round is **120.** For **varnish/lacquer finishes**: The maximum grit to use in last sanding round is **150**

Sanding Equipment

For the best end result you'll have to use (hire if necessary) a professional **belt-sander** and edge-sander. As the name suggests, a belt-sander has a continuous (or endless) belt, or rather continuous (or endless) sanding paper - called a Belt cloth. These belts are very easy to 'wrap' around the drum of the sander (1 minute tops), but most importantly will give the smoothest results on your floor.

Most DIY hire centres can only supply you with the (much lighter) drum-sander. Drum sanders have sheets of sanding paper, that have to be wrapped around the drum and fixed firmly in place with a metal bar. This metal bar, when not attached correctly will create shatter marks all over your floor. The problem is that those shatter marks will mostly only show up AFTER you applied the finish product (varnish or HardWaxOil).

Trying to remove these marks with a rotary sander will create another problem: circular marks in your floor.

Restoring Original Floorboards or Parquet Floors

More and more original wooden floors are discovered (or re-discovered) underneath carpets. Restoring these usually also means sanding off the old layer of finish. Please check our chapter on repairing/restoring your original floor, for more tips and advice.

Which Oil (HardWaxOil or Single Oil) to Use when

Question:
Do all oiled floors look orangy, I am trying to get a biscuit coloured floor with an oiled finish but can't find one.
Any help ....

Answer:
Normally only pine boards turn orangy, when applying a natural finish. Oak tends to turn honey coloured, a typical characteristic of Oak. HardWaxOil does come in various colours, and when choosing one it's always best to try the colour out (both coats) on a little left-over piece.

There are many different wood types around. Oak is still, both in the UK and many other European countries, the most commonly used species for wooden flooring.

Why Oil and a little Bit of History

Oil, more than varnish and lacquer, will bring out your wood's natural character.

Do note that every species will mature over time:
Oak will have its characteristic Honey colour and Pine can easily turn orange. If you are not in favour of this natural mature colour, you can opt for a coloured (HardWax) Oil. Some colours, like 'Golden Oak' will prevent - in most cases - the ugly orange look of pine.
You can request the leaflet on maturing of wood-species, created by our Design Manufacturer, from our website. It contains over 20 species with images showing the wood freshly installed and how it changes in colour over 2 years.

In earlier days it was quite normal to finish a floor with a chemical deep sealer, and then to apply two coats of carnauba wax. Because of changing VOC (Volatile Organic Compounds) regulations, this sealer is no longer allowed.

Manufacturers, like Osmo and Blanchon, have created a HardWaxOil with natural ingredients. This has replaced the old method, is better for the environment, and saves time for the installers.

HardWaxOil for Oak and Other European Species

Natural HardWaxOil will bring out the most character of any light coloured wood species.

HardWaxOil is a two-in-one product: Oil - which penetrates the wood - for long term protection, and wax for the wear and tear layer - to protect the wood from dirt and drips.

Easy to apply - do read the instructions and our chapter on Most Important Issues of Sanding - with an excellent and long lasting result.

It is available in various "natural" colours which, if you want, can be toned down by applying the first coat with the colour oil, followed with a second coat of natural. Always apply the coloured coat first to give the colour pigment the best chance to "stain" your wood.

Tropical Species

These darker species are mostly more oily than their European counterparts.

Applying a natural HardWaxOil might give a patchy result due to this oily nature: the oil in the HardWaxOil will not penetrate as well as it should due to the combination with the more solid wax in the product.

Euku Oil 1 (deep sealer) is a better solution. The thin oil penetrates the wood for its long term protection without any problems but is not a wear and tear layer on its own (protection against drips and spillages). For this you need to apply a normal maintenance product like the Leha StepStop to create this wear and tear layer.
In a sense you are creating your own HardWaxOil but then in a two step method instead of a two-in-one product.

Our experience with both finish types **on tropical wood species shows that Euku Oil and StepStop do tend to give a better** result than HardWaxOil .

Although Euku Oil is also available with colour pigments, why would you want to colour a tropical wood? Tropical wood is often chosen for its own rich and warm colour appearance, and in our eyes changing this would be a shame. But that just our opinion of course!

MAINTENANCE OF WOODEN FLOORS

Maintenance of wooden floors

Simple Maintenance Tips

Question:
We are about to lay a wooden floor in our dining room - which gets a lot of through traffic . I know you recommend hardwax, but I prefer a finish which has a sheen. When we lived in the Far East, parquet floors were waxed regularly and then buffed to a shine. Is this possible with the wax you recommend? I don't mind the work - I found the movement of pushing a manual floor 'bumper' (as they were called there) good exercise and therapeutic.

Answer:
You can get a shine on a wood floor that has been treated/pre-finished with HardWaxOil, when you polish (buff) the floor after applying hardwax or wax polish with our eco-friendly 7 kg weighing buffing block (which I think is the same, or works on the same principle as the manual floor 'bumper' you have been used to).

Three Categories of Care

A wooden floor is one of the few robust floor coverings that becomes even more beautiful over time, and responds to every little bit of TLC you bestow on it.

Besides being a warm, beautiful and durable product, wooden flooring is very easy to keep clean and to maintain. Like ceramic tiles, wooden flooring is a hard floor covering. Any dust or dirt will stay on top of the flooring and will not penetrated into the layers beneath, as might happen with soft floor coverings (like carpets). This feature also makes wooden flooring a good anti-allergy choice.

To make sure that you will keep enjoying the floor in the years to come, we want to give you a few practical tips on the best ways to maintain your floor.

Maintenance can be divided in three categories, namely:

1. Preventative maintenance.
2. Minor, regular maintenance.
3. Major maintenance.
   (If necessary, a difference will be made in maintenance per finishing coat.)

Preventative Maintenance

Prevention is nothing more than taking measures to avoid scratching, wears, expansion etc.

Preventative maintenance is the same for solid wood, wood engineered, cork or melamine floors.

For example:
- Placing mats at the external entrances in the room.
- Fitting felt under the legs of the sofa, chairs and tables.
- Heavy furniture needs to be lifted, not pushed.
- Don't place porous flower pots or vases on the floor.
- Stiletto's/spiked heels are safe provided that they aren't damaged.
- Prevent extreme humidity or dry atmosphere in the room.
- Remove any spilled liquid immediately (e.g. due to watering the plants or cleaning the windows).
- Remove any spilled washing powder immediately with dry cloth, or vacuum cleaner (especially for waxed floors).

During icy or snowy winters, your wooden floor might need extra protection against salt and grit.

Minor, Regular Maintenance

With minor, regular maintenance, it's important to note the difference between lacquered and waxed/ oiled floors. If you're not sure what type of finish was originally used, you can try to determine this - in most cases - as follows:
In an inconspicuous area (a corner, or behind a door), apply two drops of water. If, within ten minutes, white spots appear under the drops of water, the floor has a wax/oil finish. (To remove the white spots, gently rub the spots with 000 steel wool dampened with wax.) If the finish does not flake from scratching with a coin, and white spots do not appear from the drops of water, the floor has a surface (lacquered/varnished) finish.
 (If the floor is very old/battered the whole finish layer might have gone and drops of water will turn it very dark, then it is high time to light sand the floor to remove any residue of the old finish and apply a brand new finish)

Varnished, lacquered floors.

Minor maintenance for lacquered floors:

- Remove dirt and dust by vacuum cleaner, sweeping (soft broom) or wiping.
- Clean the floor regularly with a damp cloth, and possibly with a soft, natural soap.
- Remove persistent marks with parquet cleaner, or parquet polish (normally contains also a natural detergent).
- Treat the floor, especially the areas of heavy use, approximately 4 times a year with floor polish according to instructions. Sometimes the floor needs to be cleaned with a polish remover (according to instructions) which removes the old layers of floor polish.
- Never use steel wool or scourers.

Waxed/ oiled floors.

Minor maintenance for waxed/ oiled floors:

- Remove dirt and dust by vacuum cleaner, sweeping (soft broom) or wiping.
- Clean the floor regularly with a damp cloth (only use water).
- Remove persistent marks with wood floor cleaner (normally contains also some polish).
- Treat new floors within one-month, at half a year, and at one year with hard wax or wax polish (according to instructions). After this, treat the floor with wax or wax polish once or twice a year. The areas of heavy use (and where the floor looks "dry") need to be treated more frequently.
- When the floor gets too greasy, and/ or the wax too grey, the floor can be cleaned with a wax remover (according instructions), and then treated with wax or wax polish. The remover dissolves and removes the wax/polish.

See our range of Maintenance Products, or our maintenance service available in the East Kent area.
There is a 100% guarantee on our genuine cast-iron buffing blocks.

Major Maintenance

For major maintenance solid wood, wood engineered, cork and bamboo floors must be sanded and lacquered (or oiled/sealed).
Sanding restores an uneven, rough or weathered surface to an even, smooth and clean finish again.

Varnished, lacquered floors.

Where the lacquered layer is damaged (dark spots visible after cleaning the floor with a damp cloth), parts of the floor can be sanded lightly and lacquered again. However, this could easily result in a patchy looking area - especially when new finish overlaps the old finish. When needed, e.g. after heavy damages to a large part of the lacquer layer, the whole floor can be sanded and lacquered again. After sanding you can opt for a new finish of HardWaxOil, or colour oil instead of lacquer.

Waxed/ oiled floors.

If minor maintenance of the waxed/-oiled floor is postponed for too long, it's very easy to sand areas locally and to apply a new HardWaxOil finish without a patchy result.

TROUBLESHOOTING

Troubleshooting
[Extra information is available on our website]

Throughout this manual we've described the most common situations and methods, telling you - well, advising you really - how to tackle many issues before, during and after the installation of your wood floor. What to note, what to do, and perhaps most importantly what not to do. We're confident it will have given you a good insight into the task, and helped you realise that installing a wooden floor is not exactly rocket science.

This manual has evolved because of the questions we received from wood floor enthusiasts, on all aspects regarding selecting, installing and maintaining wooden floors.

However, as you will have read at the beginning of almost every chapter, situations and circumstances can differ for each home and for every wooden floor. In the same way that each wooden board has its own character given by nature, every house and even every room or area can have its own individual character.

This chapter contains (random) questions and answers on different situations, and in some cases unexpected problems during or after installation. We hope it will give you a further insight in what to expect, and how to confidently solve the same or similar situations in your own home.

If you have question yourself, drop by our website - www.wood-you-like.co.uk - where you'll find a link to the special "Ask Free Advice" page. You can submit your question there.

Can I Prevent the Wood from Changing Colour?

Question:
I am laying an unusual floor in my kitchen/diner. It's yellow balau, 145mm plank, screwed and plugged. I know this is usually an exterior decking wood but I like the grain structure so much I'm doing it indoors, and I've hand picked the planks to be particularly detailed.

The wood tends to darken when exposed to sunlight, and sections of the floor will be exposed to direct sunlight. What product would you recommend to stop this happening? Previously I've used hardwood oil which made the wood look fabulous but that balau floor wasn't subjected to sunlight.

Answer:
To be honest I don't think anything could stop this natural process besides hanging some 'blinds' in your windows to soften the direct sunlight, and thereby slow the process.

Any other product might also spoil the natural character in grain and colour which your wooden floor has now. Sorry, we cannot change the laws of natural chemical reactions, nor the laws of physics, wood will mature when exposed to (sun)light.

Why Not?

Question:
Why do you not recommend maple or beech to be installed with underfloor heating?

Answer:
Both Maple and Beech are known as 'nervous' woods, meaning they can shrink and expand up to 7mm per meter wide. There is a high risk that this will happen, especially on floors with Underfloor Heating, and that's why it's not recommended to use these wood species. Oak shrinks and expands only 3mm per meter wide in comparison.

Hope this makes it clearer.

Looking Odd?

Question:
I'm going to lay solid oak 18mm thick 120mm wide into a lounge 8x4 meters, and I would like to lay the boards length ways parallel. Now the tricky part is the lounge is accessed from the hallway which is quite large and if I lay parallel in the lounge then it is going to be short lengths in the hall. Which is going to look odd when you enter the front door?

Answer:
In situations like this we always advise our clients to treat every room (hallways included) separately. In our opinion it looks best when the boards are installed length ways to give the best look when you enter your home. Install a threshold in the doorway from the hall to the lounge, and install the lounge as planned. This will give you the best results, especially when the door to the lounge is normally closed.

Adding Support

Question:
We've just taken out an old dilapidated wooden floor and have replaced the old joists. I want to lay a new solid wood 18mm walnut floor and wondered whether I should do this directly onto the joists, or if it would be better to lay a plywood subfloor on to the joists first? I'm assuming that having a plywood subfloor would give additional strength and reduce wastage, are there other advantages? Finally, what would be the minimum thickness plywood that I could use for this (joists at 400mm ctrs)?

Answer:
As long as your walnut floorboards can connect with at least 3 joists, you can install your new floor directly onto them. If that's not the case you'll have to use 18mm plywood - 18mm being the minimum thickness that any flooring materials need to be to have load-bearing strength.

Additional question:
Regarding the thickness of the ply, would I not be able to reduce that (I was thinking 6mm), given that there will be some strength in my 18mm walnut boards, which will be nailed through the ply into the joists?

Answer:
Is possible, but again only when each walnut floorboard connects with at least 3 joists. But then if that was the case it would be 'overkill' to install plywood.

Additional information:
That's part of my dilemma, I expect to be contacting with just 2 joists, hence I was thinking a 6mm ply underneath would give sufficient additional integrity. Have you an opinion on that?

Answer:
Better safe than sorry in this case. You have to have a load-bearing structure on your joists. That's either the floorboards connecting with 3 joists (which is the problem, it seems, as they don't) or 18mm thick plywood and install your floorboards on top of that (floating, glued down or nailed into the plywood).

You really can't risk this I'm afraid. 6mm plywood in this case isn't enough to make your floor load-bearing.

Double Glueing?

Question:
When glueing onto a concrete floor is it advisable to pvac the grooves as well?

Answer:
When fully glueing a wood floor to a concrete underfloor there is really no need to glue the T&G's too. It's only advisable if you are installing in areas where there's more risk of moisture or spillages, such as kitchens, utility areas, bathrooms or toilets.

Can you Choose for Me?

Question:
What size parquet blocks, and what parquet pattern, would you recommend for the proportions of my flat?
I am based in xxx in a purpose built 1930's 2-bed ground floor flat. The largest room in my flat is about 4x4 m square, ceiling height 2.4m. My choice is a natural light oak parquet flooring for all rooms except kitchen and bathroom.

Answer:
In our opinion the choice in pattern of parquet flooring is down to personal taste, but often the simple patterns work best. We have installed many herringbone patterns in all types and styles of homes. Based on the measurements provided of the largest room, a standard single herringbone might suit you best: Oak prime or rustic 10 x 70 x 284 or 355mm.
Prime grade means no knots, and hardly any colour differences between the individual blocks. Rustic means small knots, and some colour differences between the blocks, making the floor more 'lively'.

On concrete underfloors we recommend the installation of an Oak mosaic subfloor (7-fingers by 7-fingers tiles of Industrial grade) to create a stable and smooth surface for the pattern to be installed on. The blocks are glued and pinned down, creating one solid and very sound-insulating beautiful floor.

Can I Sand a Floating Floor?

Quick question - Can I sand a solid strip floor if I install it by floating it on Elastilon?

(Quick) answer:
We would think so, as long as the wood floor is properly installed on the Elastilon.

How to Bond a Floor to an Uneven Concrete Floor

Question:
I need to lay oak tongue and grooved floor boards on an uneven concrete floor. Would like to know what will be the best way of bonding it as I don't have head room to put ply down first.

Answer:
It all depends really on how uneven your concrete floor is. Bonding it fully with adhesive is not recommended in this case anyway. If the unevenness isn't that bad (or widely spread) installing the floor floating (only when your boards are wider than 100mm) could be a solution. Use some extra underlayment in places where the floor dips. But as said before, this only works if there are not too many dips or 'hills' in your concrete floor. Leveling it out with a compound might be the only alternative.

Making a Space look More Spacious

Question:
I live in a small apartment of 60 square meters. It is part of an old farmhouse on the second floor just under the roof. I want to have wooden flooring in my living room, bedroom and kitchen. The living room has 2 big balcony doors with a width of 2 meters each. Therefore, the living area is light. I want the same flooring for all the three rooms.

Because the apartment is small, I would like your advice as to which type of wood, pattern, colour and finish I should choose so that the space looks bigger and more spacious? What should I definitely avoid doing?

Answer:
I can only give you some pointers I'm afraid, not knowing or seeing the actual situation.

Oak is always a good and safe bet. It's a light wood but still has loads of character, which would suit the old farmhouse. I would suggest a rustic grade over a prime/premium grade - the latter could be too bland and boring here.

You mention the living room has 2 big balcony doors, letting in the most light. If the doors are on the shortest 'wall' of the room, it's best to install the boards in the direction of the light. This will bring out the grain, colour and character of any wood type best.

Things to avoid include very wide boards, as they will make a 'square' room look very strange. In a long, narrow area small strips, like wood-engineered 3-strip , will make the room look wider. Avoid narrow bevelled single strips in those areas, and we'd also advise steering clear of dark colours.

Carpet as Underlayment?

Question:
Hi, I'm going to lay an oak laminate flooring in my hallway. I have a carpet down at the moment, which is not very thick, but has quite a smooth texture. Would I be able to lay laminate over it, and it could be used as an underlay for the laminate?

Answer:
I'm afraid the answer is NO. You should never use carpet, or old carpet underlay, underneath a hard floor covering. Not only is it a different type of "underlayment" to that which you should use when installing wooden or laminate flooring, just think of all the little bugs, house mites, etc., still in the carpet or carpet underlayment. No matter how well or often you vacuum clean, they will still be there! Bugs and house mites love warm and humid conditions - so you'd be creating the perfect breeding circumstances for them.

Remove carpet and carpet underlayment, vacuum clean the bare underfloor thoroughly, and use proper underlayment especially made for wooden or laminated flooring. This will give you the best results.

Wood Strips, Concrete and DPM Underlayment?

Question:
I have found some reclaimed maple flooring, which I would like to fit in my kitchen. It will be going over a 50 year old concrete floor, which is nicely level.

I have just read your advice about using a DPM underlayment, and then floating the floor with the T&G glued. This sounds great, but I wanted to check that it would work if the strips of solid wood are only 2 1/4" wide? If not, what would you suggest?

Answer:
The floating installation method is only suitable for floorboards wider than 100mm (4 inches). Your strip floor can best be installed fully bonded: i.e. glueing the strips to the concrete using a flexible adhesive.

Floating on Joists?

Question:

Hi, we are installing a "wet" underfloor heating system, in between joists, on the 1st floor of a barn conversion. This system consists of insulation, foil reflective layer & joist hangers that hold the pipes in between each joist. We want to put an engineered oak flooring over this but are unsure how to do it . Should we install the floor floating directly on to the joists, or secret nail it to the existing joists? We are looking at 21/22mm boards.

Answer:

It's best to install the 21mm thick wood-engineered boards nailed to the joists. Every board should connect with at least 3 joists, which then doesn't have to end on a joist. The joists should not be further apart than 35 - 40cm and you should use at least 50mm long nails.

To Brush or Not to Brush

Question:

I am currently looking for an engineered oak floor. Your website has been very informative, however I have a question: Is there a difference between the amount of dirt that can get left on an oak floor which has a brushed finish, and a normal smooth finish? It would seem that there may be a possibility for dirt to become trapped in the grain, and then need "scrubbing" out? Any advice on this would be very useful in helping me to decide on my floor!

Answer:

In the early days of brushed floors this was indeed a concern, because the brushing left rather deep gorges in the surface.
Nowadays, however, it's a very gently brushing that takes place, enhancing the character of the wood without making into a gathering place for dirt. Hope this diminishes your worries.

Random Pattern?

Question:

I have bought some character grade oak, which has come in 5 widths (150, 170, 190, 230, 270, 330mm). I have two rooms to floor on concrete, and will have them latex self leveled, and have Treatex wax oil.
1. What is the best knot and split filler to use?

2. Is there a specific pattern to use the widths in?

3. The carpenter has only layed the 'perfect' stuff before ready filled and lacquered, this is more of a challenge - any advice?

Answer:

Thank you for your questions. 230mm, 270mm and 330mm are very wide to be honest.

Don't use them next to each other. And no, there is not really a pattern to follow. The best original result will come from a random use of the widths.

Lecol7500 is a good filler. When you sand the installed floor you'll have to collect the sand dust to mix with the product.

And the only advice we can give is take your time, make the correct preparations, ensure the concrete is level and dry, and check the quality of the materials. Has one board width differences, meaning wider at one end than the other end? If that is the case with a number of boards, then getting a perfect fit will be impossible (and filling will not always solve this).

How Often do I have to Re-oil an Oiled Floor?

Question:
We have parquet floor and I want to sand it and treat it. If I went for the HardWaxOil you recommend how often would I have to oil it? Is it every 6 months or so? I want a treatment that means I don't have to work at it too often, if possible.

Also, how much oil would I need to buy? What areas do the 1L and 2.5L tins cover please?

Answer:
The benefit of HardWaxOil is that you don't have to re-oil it, only apply a suitable maintenance product every 5 - 6 months to keep the floor healthy and protected against dirt and drips. Easy maintenance indeed!

As for coverage of the HardWaxOil - if you ever need to re-sand your floor: 1 ltr covers app. 10 sq m in two coats, 2.5 ltr covers 25 sq m.

Changing Directions in a L-Shaped Room

Question:
I want to lay a wooden floor in my new conservatory. The conservatory is "L" shaped approx 6.8m length on one side and 7.1m on the other side with a width of approx 3m. Therefore the overall area is about 32.7m2.

I would like the "planks" to lay lengthwise in both sides of the conservatory which would mean a 90deg turn or a cut at 45deg across the planks. Would you be able to supply planks with a pre-cut 45degree tongue and groove to do the job?

Answer:
I'm afraid what you ask for (T&G on 45 degree cuts) is not available. In the event you do change direction, both areas do need an expansion gap where they meet. We suggest you use a flat Oak strip to cover this expansion gap in the most unobtrusive way.

In an L-shaped room like yours, another alternative would be to install all boards diagonally. This does mean more saw-waste though, but gives the most aesthetic and eye pleasing result.

Oil-Based Lacquer? Is it Oil, Lacquer or a Combination of Both?

Question:
We have seen an engineered wood product which has an "oil-based lacquer" finish. We are unsure what this is. Is it more oil or more lacquer? We have a dog, and two teenage children, and want a floor that improves with age in its looks, not deteriorates. We aim to put a wooden floor down in our hall and dining room.

Answer:
Oil-based lacquer is indeed a lacquer with the appearance of an oiled finish, but not with the benefits of it.

In your situation I would definitely opt for a normal oiled finished (pre-oiled or finished on site with HardWaxOil), as this will become more beautiful over time (when regular maintenance is applied, once every 5 - 6 months, the same goes for lacquered floors). It won't show wet shoe prints as easily as lacquer will, and on the occasions when it suffers some minor damage it will be easier to repair without causing a "patchy" look.

When to Install Flat Beading, Before or After?

Question:
I am quite interested in the solid oak flat beading, and would like to know if the process of fitting this would be before or after the actual new flooring has been laid? The reason I ask is because I have someone booked in to fit the flooring, but have now finally come across "flat beading" (looks so much better in my opinion, as i am not in a position to remove and re add skirting). I need to ensure this gets in at the right time depending on where it fits into the installation process... basically before or after the new floor has been laid? Any help or advice here would be greatly appreciated.

Answer:
Flat Solid Oak beading is installed after the new wood floor has been installed, and is pinned down on the floor with tiny nails or with double sided tape if no little nails are available.

Your fitter should leave a sufficiently wide expansion gap between the new floor and your skirting boards (and all around the perimeter of the floor, even underneath door posts etc).

Staggering Amount of Shrinkage.

Question:
I have a question with regard to the acceptable amount of shrinkage of Marine Pine Floor boards.

We installed the 130mm wide 21mm thick floor boards, unfortunately during a relatively humid period in August *(2008)*, with some windows not yet installed.

The floor was nailed, and (again unfortunately) also partly glued between the boards. It was laid tied with one of these spring loaded tools that allow a large hammer to be applied.

Since then all boards have gradually shrank by a staggering amount. The average shrinkage per 130mm board is 4mm. Some up to 6mm. As a result we obviously have hideously big gaps, enhanced by the fact that in some cases the glue holds the boards together, resulting in some gaps to take the movement of a number of boards. The biggest resulting gaps are more than 10mm with the tongue exiting the groove.

Does all this mean that the supplier provided timber that must have had a unacceptably high moisture content?

Prior to laying the boards we had them unwrapped 1 week before. They were stored in the space but obviously the lack of windows meant it wasn't indoor climate.

Answer:
I'm really sorry, but in this case that amount of shrinkage was to be expected. Pine, and any other wood, should only be installed - and stored a few days/weeks before installation - in a room that is wind and weather tight.

August was indeed very humid, and the wood floor "acclimatised" to outside conditions. Now, when your home is wind and weather tight, plus the very low air humidity (inside due to heating as well as outside now with the "cold-snap" we're having - *2008*), the wood can do nothing else than release moisture to its surroundings. In fact, as soon as your home was wind and weather tight your wood floor started to acclimatise to its normal surroundings.
Pine can have a normal moisture content of 15% - versus Oak which should always be supplied between 9 - 11% moisture - but as with all wooden products that is at one point in time. Did you check the moisture content of your wood floor when it arrived? If not, I'm afraid you can't go back to your suppliers with this complaint.

I know it will be a pain, but the best thing to do would be to lift the floor and re-install it. Make sure the humidity in your home stays between 45 - 65% (during these cold-snaps that could be difficult), and leave wider expansion gaps around in order to prevent extra expansion when the humidity start to rise again, in Spring and Summer.

Sorry I don't have better news for you, but the correct preparations are one of the most important issues for the best and long lasting result.

Small Bathroom, Small Budget - is Wood Flooring Feasible?

Question:

I'm thinking about installing timber flooring in a small bathroom, with floor area of 1.3m wide x 2.5m long. The base is good condition, stable, chipboard on glu-lam joists (it's a timber frame house circa 5 years old) with the door and window facing each other in the shorter walls. The budget for the project is circa £200, and I would like to see a dark finish timber.

Firstly is it possible to recommend a project given the tight budget? (I hate photocopy-timber laminate finishes!)

Secondly, even if it is possible to meet these parameters, I'm concerned about how the fixings for the WC & Basin pedestal in the flooring substrate will affect the expansion / contraction of the flooring. Would you drill over-sized holes through the new flooring to ensure that the screws don't effectively "fix" the flooring tight?

Answer:

Wood-engineered in bathrooms is very feasible. The best way, if it's possible, is always to remove the toilet pan and pedestal before installation takes place. Leave a gap in the floor wide enough for the pan and the pedestal to "rest" on again. Seal the floor around the pan/pedestal with transparent silicon to prevent moisture getting in even more.

Budget wise there are darker basic wood-engineered boards available (such as Triplank Oak "Oeral"), but you would need two packs, so we're not sure if - including delivery charges - it would meet your budget.

How Uneven is Uneven?

Question:

When determining whether to put down a layer of plywood for uneven floors, how uneven is uneven? My room has floorboards which have been taken up a couple of times for central heating, etc., but they have been replaced very neatly. Is there any guide as to when you should use plywood?
Also, when laying a solid wood floor over floorboards, and plywood is put down first, do I need to use the foam underlay as well, or does the plywood do the job of the underlay?

Answer:

If your floorboards are even, you can get away with using 3mm hardboard sheets. Slightly uneven, say protruding edges, you use 6mm plywood. Very uneven, such as cupped boards, then it's 12mm plywood. Hope this gives you an indication of what you should use in your situation.

When floating a wood floor always use foam underlayment (3mm) on top of sheet material for sound insulation.

Painting a Liquid DPM?

Question:
If fitting an engineered wooden floor onto concrete, would you recommend a DPM to be painted onto the concrete, or is this not needed?

Answer:
It depends on two things. Firstly is the moisture content of the concrete 2.1% or lower? If so, no liquid DPM is needed. If the moisture content is higher than 4% then no liquid DPM will help - you'll have to wait until the moisture content is 4% or lower.

If installing the floor floating (and the above is taken care of), you should use a combi-underlayment (sound-insulation and DPM in one).

How to Re-Do a "Professional" Job

Question:
We moved into our house around three years ago, and had to replace the floor in a ground-floor living room. The floor was a suspended floor on joists with ~350 mm centres. Perhaps mistakenly, we decided to go for a solid oak floor directly onto the joists, and unfortunately, although the boards are reasonable quality, the guy who fitted them was a cowboy. He left no expansion gap, and the boards have now risen in several places. Additionally, the floor seems draughty, and the room cold.

It's probably a hopeless case, but I would like to try to lift the floor, put down a plywood subfloor, and relay them. Can you give me any advice on how to lift them, and on whether glueing to the subfloor might be a possibility - I am expecting that in lifting the boards I will get some damage to the tongue.

The boards are 21mm oaks, T&G on four sides, 110mm wide, random length. The joists are layed over a fairly shallow underfloor space (no more than 300 mm, I would say) to earth. The underfloor space is ventilated by air-bricks.

Answer:
If you plan to install plywood as a subfloor, you'll need to buy plywood at least 18mm thick so that it is load-bearing.

Lifting the existing floorboards can be done with a crow-bar. The easiest way is to start at one wall, and remove the skirting board for better access. You are right about damaging some of the T&G's, and glueing down the Oak boards to the plywood subfloor would be the best option for you. Leave sufficient wide expansion gaps: 3 - 4 mm per meter width of the room with a minimum of 10mm (a 4 meter wide room needs 15 - 16 mm gap).

You'll have to use flexible adhesive, such as Mapei P990.

Contradictory Advice (on the product!)

Question:

I've just bought some solid oak wood flooring from Homebase. On the packet it says easy to lay: tap together, glue required. The boards are 12mm thick, but when you open the pack and read the installation guide it recommends that solid boards are nailed.

Can I lay this floor as a floating floor over a good underlay and glue the t&g, or does it have to be nailed?

Answer:

Just when you thought you'd heard everything, a big retailer manages to surprise us again!

Not to sound rude, but have you confronted Homebase with this? It would seem that your guarantee, no matter how you install this floor, is rendered useless because of the contradictions in instructions.

Anyway, before we can suggest the best way to install this floor we need to know the following:

How wide are the boards, how long (and if random, how many of the shortest? more than 30%, more than 50%?) and what type of underfloor do you have?

Reply:

Before I had a chance to read your reply I used my common sense and packed the lot back to Homebase. I thought if I had tried to lay this floor, nailed or glued I would be paying for it in the long run.

Once again thanks a lot, and if anyone wants any info on wood floors I'll tell them to check out your site.

Supplier sold me Adhesive, Pack Instructions Say: Do Not Glue

Question:

Hi, I have bought some solid oak wooden flooring with tongue and groove. The supplier sold me adhesive and told me it could be laid straight on to floorboards with adhesive. The instructions tell me not to glue the long tongue and groove joint. Do I just apply glue to floorboards, lay the floor and only glue the short tongue?? Do I nail the boards or is adhesive sufficient?? Basically I need to know how to lay the flooring to achieve best results.....

Answer:

Well, that's a first for us: glueing new floorboards onto existing floorboards. If your existing boards are only even a little bit cupped or uneven the new boards will not bond with adhesive.

Take back the adhesive the supplier sold you (and tell him off for even suggesting such a method!). Due to the instructions your best bet is to use the self-adhesive underlayment, and check your existing floorboards are pretty sound and level. If you plan to install in the same direction of the existing boards, screw or staple plywood sheets first.

Wood in Music Room?

Question:
Thinking of having an engineered wood floor installed but wondered if it would take the weight of a baby grand piano. Would it not scratch the floor when continually moving the stool. There are 3 pianists in the house and all have the stool in different positions.

Answer:
If a floor can take the weight of your piano depends largely on the construction of the underfloor and/or joists. Scratches to the floor from the stool depends on the material of the bottom of the legs (rubber, wheels, plain wood), and if moving the stool happens only when adjusting height or if it's constantly "wiggled" on/with.
If needed, a protective mat can be placed underneath the stool (see-through types like those for computer chairs, and available from any quality office furniture business).

I've been Told to use DPM on Existing Floorboards

Question:
I hope to install solid oak flooring on a ground floor that has suspended wooden floorboards. I intend to put 12mm plywood to level the existing floorboards. I have been told to use excel Timbermate membrane in order to prevent any moisture rising from the ground. Do I install this on top of the existing floorboards or on top of the 12mm ply and then lay the oak flooring?

Answer
What you have been told is definitely wrong. On underfloor/subfloors that consist of wood or sheet materials, like existing floorboards and plywood, you should never install a membrane. This can cause condensation between underfloor/subfloor, and even cause rotting of the joists. If you need extra sound-insulation, select the Timbermate Duratex, not the Excel. The Duratex comes without the DPM (membrane).

Am I Paranoid? Tiny Damage to a Board I Cannot Replace

Question:
Hi! I have started a flooring project which includes a hallway, a living room and a bedroom. I am using lacquered 18mm Ipe T+G. I've just completed the hallway and now will continue to the living room. I am really paranoid as I have just noticed a very tiny thin crack on the corner of one board, this is very small crack which is about 1cm in length and only noticeable when looked at very closely. I can't take it off as it is connected to the other planks and it will require me to take of a lot of planks. I just wanted to know am

I being too paranoid over nothing, or will this affect the flooring in the long run, and if there was a way to protect it? I really appreciate your help? Thank you.

Answer:
Don't panic!
It is always a devastating feeling to see a first little bit of damage to your brand new floor, but don't worry - more will follow to add to the character of your floor. There is no way to prevent these little bits of damage anyway. Remember, carpets will also look worn over time, but the only option to bring back shine to them is to replace them - at least it's a completely different situation with wooden flooring.

The wood is still protected, and you can even disguise the crack with a suitable polish. Make sure you buy a polish that is suitable for a lacquered/varnished finish and apply a little bit on the crack.

Wide Solid Oak for More than One Room - are we Looking for Problems?

Question:
We want to install solid oak wood flooring through the kitchen, dining room, hall and sitting room, that have just been knocked together. The total area is about 80 square meters, and is made up of concrete and chipboard. The oak is 22mm thick, 200mm wide and in lengths from 1.4m to 2.4m. The wood man suggests Sika T54 will do the trick, but do you think we need to have a plywood underlay (we're pushed for height) throughout? Otherwise would you recommend engineered wood?

Answer:
Would you mind if I start with your last question? Yes, we would recommend wood-engineered floorboards if you're set on wide boards (and definitely when installing wood in kitchens). A 200mm wide solid board is very wide, and truly we would not recommend them in areas where there is more moisture.

As for going through all the rooms without installing thresholds where needed, that is also something we would not recommend. There are very nice solid Oak strips (bevelled on two sides) that can go between the doorways, so you can treat every room as a separate entity. This might also solve your two types if underfloor problem, as you can just use the appropriate underlayment for each underfloor.

What we normally do is line-up the boards in connecting rooms so that it looks as if they are continuing from one room into the other, but with the needed expansion gap and a threshold in between.

T&G versus Clic, and should I opt for Oiled? Decisions, Decisions!

Question:

We are hoping to fit a wooden floor in our hall and porch. We have done some research and found wooden engineered and solid wood planks in a clic system that appear easy to install. They also come prefinished in lacquer or wax oil. Are there any thoughts you have on this as to what to be aware of? We are going for the clic system because it will be going on a concrete floor with an underlay, and won't need glueing.

Also despite your extensive and very informative site, I am still unclear as to what maintenance is actually required on the wax oil wood. Everyone says to avoid it but it looks better in my opinion, so what actually needs doing on a daily basis and every 5-6 months? And what happens if this is not maintained. Does it only look good if it is continually buffed?

Thank you for your brilliant web site and help.

Answer:

Thank you for your question and your kind words about our website.

Click-systems can be very handy, but only - in our and many others experience - in large fairly rectangular rooms. The problem starts with narrow areas which have plenty of doors, like hallways. In those areas standard T&G is much easier to install because you don't need that specific angle to slot the last board in, which you must have with a click-system board.

In hallways, we always recommend wood-engineered floors. These are much more stable in areas where there can be more moisture and/or changes in temperature (think about opening the front door etc when it is raining).

Oiled floors are indeed nicer to look at, and easy to maintain. In the event that there is any minor damage, you can easily repair it locally without having to sand the whole floor (which you will have to do with a lacquer floor to prevent a patchy result). Another advantage of an oil floor, especially in hallways, is the fact that wet shoe prints won't show up immediately as they do on lacquered floors.

As for maintenance, a soft broom or vacuum cleaner is all that's needed for normal day to day care, and every 5 - 6 months you apply a maintenance product suitable for oiled floors. In hallways you could consider applying a maintenance product every 4 -5 months, and a clean with a suitable cleaning product (like Lecol/Leha's "Wax & Clean"), every month. The 'soap' contains not only a soft detergent, but also polish, so your cleaned floor will not dry up dull.

What happens if you don't maintain your wood floor? Well, no matter what the finish, the floor will start to look 'tired', dirty, and could even turn grey - which would be a shame considering how easy it is to maintain a natural wooden floor.

New Oak Floorboards on Existing Wood Mosaic

Question:

My husband plans to lay new solid oak flooring in our large living room (approx 50sqm). The oak flooring is 18mm depth, 150mm width with the boards varying in length between 400m up to 1800mm. We've opened the packs that it comes in, and the majority seem to be between 700mm - 1000mm.

Currently we have poor quality parquet tiles stuck to the floor, and some of the small pieces that make up the tiles are loose or missing. What is the best way to lay our new oak floor? Do we need to take all these old tiles up first to expose the old adhesive/cement, or can we lay it directly on top? Also should we nail it down or use adhesive? Many thanks.

Answer:

If you don't want to remove the existing floor and start from scratch, you can install your new solid wood floor on top of the existing parquet blocks using the floating method, on foam underlayment (DO NOT USE an underlayment that contains a DPM!) and to glue the T&G's correctly.

Loose blocks in the existing floor could be fixed back with some gripfill if there are only a few - missing blocks could be replaced with strips of wood or plywood of the same height.

Another option would be to use Elastilon Basic self-adhesive underlayment

Oops, Waited 2 weeks instead of 2 days for the Second Coat of HardWaxOil

Question:

I saw your numerous replies on DIY-not forum and hope you can help... sorry for firing a couple of random questions at you!

I have sanded down the floorboards and applied 2 coats of Blanchon satin HardWaxOil. However I may have done something rather stupid... I applied the first coat 2 weeks before the second (went on holiday - second coat went on this morning). It's only just occurred to me that the first coat may have hardened too much to allow the second to dry. It's too early to tell yet, but will I have problems? And if it won't dry, what's the solution?

Thanks in advance for your help.

Answer:

You might have a problem indeed - but only time will tell (probably rather soon, though!) Applying the second coat should happen within 48 hours of the first coat, otherwise the "grains" of the wood will rise, and a light resanding is needed.

But then again, the time lapse of 14 days might not give that much of a problem after all. Keep an eye on the drying of the floor. In normal circumstances - not too cold and/or not too high or too low air humidity - this should take no more than 8 - 10 hours. You might see some patchy areas where the wax part of the product lays on top of the floor instead of being absorbed. That is nothing to worry about.

Don't apply a third coat of HardWaxOil however, that will not improve things.

If the floor does not dry, or you see many patchy areas, you could try to buff the floor with a medium coarse pad - without applying any polish or wax to the floor first. If that doesn't give a better looking result - and it may not be immediate, so wait 1 or 2 days before condemning your effort - depending on the "problem" you can do the following:

If the floor is still wet or tacky - remove excess wax with white spirit or special wax-remover and wait a few hours, then buff with coarse pad again.

If there are still many patchy areas after using white spirit or the wax-remover, apply a liquid polish (maintenance product suitable for oiled floors) to create a new or extra wear and tear layer.

Hope this helps, give us a shout if you need further advice

Reply:
I'll see how it looks tomorrow morning - it actually seems to have started drying already. It's now tacky instead of oily, and it doesn't look too patchy yet. I think the wood type may actually help - it seems very hard and smooth anyway (not like the soft young pine boards which I sanded in another room). I'll follow your advice if it doesn't look right after a couple of days.

Thanks again for an excellent service - wish I had found your website earlier!

Wood Floors when the Priority is Acoustic Insulation

Question:
I want to put down some type of wooden floor (not laminate) in mansion flat. Priority is acoustic insulation - otherwise the managing agent will tell me to take it up. Because of problem with added height - I presume I shall have to remove existing floor boards - and lay over joists? Area is about 55 sq m, hallway and double reception room to flow into each other.

Questions - What is the best insulation to use? I presume I shall have to use some form of rigid board either as the sound insulation or in addition to it - as well as the finished product. Shall I also use something in between joists? I presume I shall have to remove all skirting boards - some already removed - and then replace.

Answer:
Most sounds travel through pipes, which means no matter what installation method you use you have to make sure that around pipes (central heating, water pipes etc) there is a wide enough expansion gap in the new wood floor.
Depending on your height restrictions, the most simple solution would be to install a quality acoustic underlayment. In your case I would suggest self-adhesive Elastilon to prevent any air gaps that might produce footfall noise.

The problem with nailing new boards onto joists is that over time, due to normal seasonal movement, the nails might start to "rub" and create creaking sounds that will be transported down.

What Should I Ask?

Question:
I have people coming to give me quotes on supplying and fitting a wooden or engineered wooden floor tomorrow.

What are the really important questions I should ask them?

The present floor is a thin screed laid over stone flags. The screed in one room is starting to break down. I want the boards to match the original flooring in the sitting room which are 7" wide and probably pine.

Answer:
Follow our 11 key questions check list and you can't go wrong. Make also sure you point out the screed that is breaking down, and ask them how they are going to tackle this. Installing the floor floating would be an option, but be aware that the defective screed could cause crackling/whispering noises once a new floor is installed on top of it.
Also remember that pine tends to turn orange when it "matures". Do they know this, do they advise a coloured finish to prevent this?
(Our "11 key questions" can be found in the online "Extras")

Is a Mat Well and Coconut Mat Recommended?

Question:
Do you recommend having a sunken door mat at the entrance to the front door in the hallway. We are hoping to lay an oak plank flooring (tongue and groove). If yes, can you purchase a trim to go round the edge where it meets the carpet? Can you have coconut mats made to measure?

Answer:
We do indeed recommend to place a mat behind the front door, but to be honest coconut or coir mats don't really work that well in removing all the moist from shoes. There are other, better suited, mats available in any carpet shops, which can be cut to size.

For trims around the mat, we would normally use end thresholds.

How many Bottles?

Question:
I want to use your Lecol PAVC wood-glue 750 gr to fit a floating bamboo floor. How much do I need? The flooring is 96mm wide & the floor is 4 x 4m. My guess is 8 bottles, is this correct?

Answer:
Thank you for your question. 4 x 4 is 16 sq m. Basing the usage of PVAC on our own experience with wider boards (189, twice as wide as yours), we would use maximum 2 bottles, so in your case I would say: 3 - 4. Eight bottles is too much, especially when - like with bamboo - the grooves are not that deep or large.

A 10mm Gap is a 10mm Gap, Not 2 x 5mm

Question:
When laying solid wood flooring, your manual recommends a minimum expansion gap of 10mm. Is this 10mm on both sides of the room, or a total expansion gap of 10mm (i.e. 5mm on each side)?

Answer:
No, it is definitely minimum 10mm all around the perimeter of the floor, not a total of 10mm in a room. Five millimeters is really not enough to cater for a wood floor's natural movement during the seasons.

Hollow Sounds - Would Foam Help?

Question:
We've had a wood floor installed recently over concrete (glued down). Now it seems the concrete was not as level as the fitter thought 'cos we've now got hollow sounds in some areas where we think the glue did not hold. The fitter is suggesting to drill little holes in some of the bevels and inject expanding foam to fill the hollows? What'd you think?

Answer:
We've heard this "solution" suggested fairly often, but DO NOT inject expanding foam underneath your floor! You have hardly any control over how much foam is injected and once it starts expanding there's absolutely no brake on it! (Once we saw the result of expanding foam inserted underneath "rocking" ceramic tiles that were installed onto plywood. Where the foam was injected "mushroom shaped" excess foam appeared and the whole area became even more unstable.)

Expanding foam is definitely a no no. Inserting pvac wood glue into drilled small holes would be a better alternative, but your fitter should have checked the levelness of the concrete better before starting the installation. Hoping that the adhesive he used to glue down the board to the uneven concrete would act like a filler is not the best way to tackle a known problem.

Filling Dips with Underlayment - the Right Way

Question:

Hi there, I am about to lay a 20mm thick engineered T&G floor over the old existing floorboards, with a soundproof underlay between them. The shop told me that it could be laid as a floating floor with glue. Not knowing a lot about laying floors I didn't realise just how flat the existing floor needs to be in order to not need nailing of the new floor. My question is just how much uneven variation can I really get away with on the existing floor before I need to nail instead? The shop says the underlay will absorb differences of up to 3mm. (Great site, wish I'd found this before embarking on the project!!) Thanks.

Answer:

An underfloor, no matter of which material, should be as level as possible (meaning not too many deeps dips or high 'bumps') but a wood floor can tackle a gentle slope (in one direction) of maximum 3mm per meter. Especially your 20mm thick engineered can handle a lot before it goes bouncing around. What we normally do is have extra underlayment (of different thickness) at hand to 'level' out small areas of dips, but be careful. Only do it if you can slide the extra bit of underlayment underneath the floorboard - if you have to lift it up to get underneath, the problem will travel down the row. Hope this helps

Additional information about dips or bows:

Check if it is indeed a dip or if your board is bowed. Use a spirit-level and place this on the board that's giving you trouble. Before you add any extra material press the board down, and if the spirit level indicates your board is now level it is an indication you don't have a dip at all but a slightly bowed board. Most times this will sort itself out when this board is connected with other boards (rows). Best practice: install one or two boards without glueing the T&G yet to see if the "problem" board becomes more level. If so, remove the test-boards and continue with the installation. If not: replace the problem board with another one to see if that makes sufficient difference.

If however the spirit-level shows your board is indeed straight you do have a dip and follow as explained in our answer.

Caution: this trick of the trade will not replace the preparations you should take when your concrete floor is of rather bad quality filled with dips and hills and should only be used sparsely.

Cats! Always there Where and When you Don't Need Them!

Question:

Hi Karin, Followed advice from your good selves which has not been flawed so far. Sanding pine boards finishing with 100 grit. Applied Blanchon coloured HWO as per instructions just finished last night, only to find that between the sanding process and the oiling process our cat had walked on the bare pine with wet feet. These paw prints were not visible until the HWO was applied but now we have some well defined paw prints in numerous places. They feel slightly raised to the touch.

My question is will they fade over time or should I resort to the wire wool treatment?"

Answer:
It's always the same with these nice creatures: they hide away right up to the moment you absolutely do not want them on your floor! (Happened to us right after applying a coloured oil once, and we learned it is absolutely not recommended to try to chase the cat from a wet floor!).

It is best to lightly sand the effected areas, careful you do not put too much pressure on it to avoid "closing-up" of the grain. Then apply the second coat of HardWaxOil - after vacuum cleaning of course - according the instructions.

The paw prints might slightly shine through in the beginning, that will fade over time and you can "speed" this up by applying a wax polish after the HardWaxOil is fully cured = 2 weeks.

Hope this helps. One last thing... Keep the cat firmly out of the way until you're finished ;-))

When it Comes to Doorways?

Question:
Hi we are going to lay solid wood flooring from the hall into the kitchen, then put new skirting boards on so we don't have to use any trimming around the edges, but I'm wondering what do we do when it comes the door ways? How do we do the edging in the frame of the doors, as we obviously can not put skirting there! Please Help!

Answer:
The simplest and neatest way is to undercut the door-posts and architraves to slide the floor underneath. Make sure you also allow for expansion gaps underneath the doorpost, so don't cut it too shallow.

"Going with the Light"?

Question:
Hi, i am going to lay an engineered click oak floor in my lounge which is 6mtrs square. There are windows on the north and south walls and the door is on the east side. Which way do you recommend laying the boards, should it be from north to south to catch the light on the boards? Thank you

Answer:
You're spot on! Always try to go "with the light" especially when you have bevelled floorboards. This to prevent false shadows when the sun is shining, plus the grain of the wood will show its best character this way.

Double Problems - Tiles, Bitumen and the Need to Glue

Question:
Hi, I want to lay 23 m2 of solid oak T&G flooring, the existing floor is a concrete one, with hard vinyl tiles layed down on bitumen. What would you recomend? If I take up the vinyl tiles I know it will be a real pain getting up the bitumen, but if i lay the oak floor floating, will I have problems with it coming apart?

Answer:
If the vinyl tiles are stuck down well, the underfloor fairly level and your solid Oak boards are wider than 100mm then we would install a floor in this circumstances floating on a combi-underlayment, glueing all T&G's correctly. Hope this helps.

Reply 1:
Hi, thanks for the quick response. Unfortunately the floor is a solid oak,18mm thick, by 83mm wide random plank length, so I assume laying it floating is a no-no. Would it be possible to glue it to the existing vinyl tiles, provided they were stuck down well?

Answer:
We're afraid not. The structure of the tiles will not allow the adhesive to bond correctly. Alternatively you could screw plywood on top of it first, and then glue the wood floor on to that.

Reply 2:
Hi Karin, thank you again. I've decided to fetch up the existing vinyl tiles. I'm either going to use Elastilon strong over a DPM, or use a primer and a liquid batten such as sikabond T2. Which method would you recommend? And do I have to remove all the bitumen residue from the concrete before using a primer? Many thanks for your patience!

Answer:
The more bitumen you remove the better it is. Using Elastilon also has the advantage of tackling minor unevenness's in the underfloor, but for the rest it is personal preference what to use.

Defective Materials or Wrong Method?

Question:
Had 5/8" floating engineered maple installed. Instructions say to use T&G glue, but I found out it was NOT used during the installation. It has now been about 5 months and the laminate layer is cupping and un-adhering to the lower portion of the plank on some boards. Is this just defective flooring or could it be a result of the glue not being used. Thanks!

Answer:
Delaminating is due to failing bonding between toplayer and backing and when this happens it is normally covered in the guarantee of the product. Has nothing to do

with not glueing the T&G's together. You should contact the company your bought the product from and inform them of the problem. They must send someone out to check the problem. Hope this helps

Do you have a question?

Remember:

If you have question yourself, drop by our website www.wood-you-like.co.uk where you will find a link to the special "Ask Free Advice" page and submit your question there.

Things Not to Expect from your Wood Floor

Don't expect:

1. A **floor without** (tiny) **gaps** between the floorboards, or within the parquet pieces. Although your new floor may start tight together, as a natural product is will continue to absorb and release moisture. This natural process will cause the floor to expand and shrink from season to season, resulting in gaps between some of the boards in your floor. Some colours, such as white, will show this more than others.

2. A **floor that will not indent**. In spite of the term hardwood, most floors will indent under high heel traffic (specially when heels are damaged), or dropping hard or sharp materials onto it. The finish that is applied will not prevent the dents.

3. A **monochromatic floor**. Wood, as a natural product, varies from piece to piece, and from board to board. Remember, it's not fabricated (like Melamine Laminate flooring), it's milled from a tree, and will have grain and colour variations consistent with the grade and species of the wood selected.

4. A **dust-free finish**. When we/you apply the finish to the floor in your home, it's not possible to achieve a "clear room" environment. Some dust will fall into the freshly applied material.

Remember that furniture, cabinets, doors etc are fabricated in a factory under ideal conditions, and that they contain any number of different pieces of wood. When your floor is "fabricated" in your own home it is made up of 10 to a thousand individual pieces.

Remember also that your floor is never to be duplicated... it's a truly custom wooden floor of your own!

Kind Regards

Wood You Like Ltd
Karin Hermans / Ton Slooven

Where to Find more Information

Wood You Like has an expansive website, and many other wood-guides you could benefit from.

Website areas

Go to www.wood-you-like.co.uk with the various sections:

About Wood You Like, and our quality ranges

The Wood Flooring Knowledge base

The Wood Floor Guides

The Wood Floor Manuals

The interactive Frequently Asked Questions and News Site (ask your question in the "comment-box")

The Secure Webshop

Subscribe to our newsletter and receive news on our 'Newsletter Readers Only' special offer

The Site map

Contact Details

Wood You Like Ltd
www.wood-you-like.co.uk
Tel: 01233 713725 (Charing, Kent UK)
email: info@wood-you-like.co.uk

Opening hours:
Tuesday - Saturday: 9.30am - 5pm (please avoid the notorious school run between 3.10 - 3.25pm)
Sunday & Monday: afternoons, times may vary - please call to make sure we're in or make an appointment.

Members of the British Wood Flooring Association (BwfA) no: C200826
FSC retailer ID code: FSC-GBR-1019

Registered in England and Wales.
Company no: 04584873 Registered office: Roper Yard, Roper Road, Canterbury, Kent CT2 7EX
VAT reg: 826129824
Quotations, transactions and deliveries are subject to our terms and conditions of trading

EXTRAS: ORIGINAL PARQUET - MOSAIC FLOORS

Extras: Original parquet - mosaic floors

3 Easy Steps to Clean and Maintain Your Design Parquet Floor - or any other wooden floor

[Extra info available online - www.woodmanual.co.uk]

Hidden Treasure Exposed

What is a nicer surprise than to remove the carpet from a room in your home and to discover a valuable original parquet floor is hiding beneath it! Especially when you consider that installing a brand new parquet floor costs around £125.00 - £145.00 per sq m. And that's just for a simple herringbone or basket weave pattern.

Your new discovery will at least need some TLC to bring back its grand lustre it had before it was 'covered-up'. Follow our "3 easy steps" below, and you will start enjoying your valuable, easy to clean and anti-allergic original parquet floor in no time at all.

Where needed we've listed quality products (types and/or brands) we recommend you use for the best result.

If your floor is missing some blocks, has damaged blocks – damages from plumbing work come to mind - or you notice areas where the blocks no longer stuck firmly down on the underfloor, see our guide "**7 Easy Steps to Repair/Restore your Parquet Floor**". But 9 times out of 10 some extra TLC is the only thing needed. If we're honest, sanding down an authentic 'old-fashion' design parquet removes much of its original appealing character.

Step 1: Cleaning Carpet Residue, old layers of Wax and old Dirt
Carpet Residue

Depending on how long the carpet has been down, and how this was installed, you'll no doubt find some degree of old carpet, underlayment, and carpet grippers sticking to your wooden floor. Some old fashioned 'elbow grease' has to be applied to remove most of this without damaging your valuable discovery.

Carpet grippers should be remove with care by gently lifting the gripper out of the wood. Stick a chisel under one end of the gripper. and by *careful* wriggling it should come off without damaging your wooden floor. Or use a screwdriver to lift the staples out of the gripper first - that way when you have to use more force only the gripper itself takes the brunt of it.

Tear of as much of the carpet underlayment as possible manually - consider it a labour of love. Don't use a damaged metal scraper to remove the last bits of foam, instead make sure that if you use a sharp object that the edge is straight. Hard plastic scrapers might work better. As last resort, use Mineral Spirit or lacquer thinner - but always read the instructions carefully before you use these chemicals. Wear gloves and face-protection, and make sure there is sufficient ventilation in the room!

Old Wax Layers

If you notice a dark, sticky substance on the floor, your original parquet floor has been treated with too much wax in the past.

'Wax-removers' from most brands only work on newly installed floors, not really on wax that has been covered over for years. In our experience using White Spirit still works best to remove these old layers. Again, when using chemicals always read the instructions carefully, wear gloves and face-protection, and make sure the room is well ventilated.

Old Dirt

After you removed the carpet you will notice a layer of dust and dirt, no matter how well or often the carpet has been vacuum cleaned. Either use a soft broom or decent vacuum cleaner to remove it. A cylinder cleaner with brush nozzle is preferable, as the wheels of an upright cleaner could scratch your floor when too much pressure is applied. For reluctant dirt use a (clean) hard brush to shift it.

After this rigorous treatment most dirt will have gone. To finish the cleaning part of the job use a natural detergent (Wax & Clean - cleaning soap) diluted in water to remove the remaining dirt. Don't use washing-up liquid, that might be good for your hands but is not suitable for wooden floors! Wash the floor with a small quantity of water (well-wrung out cloth), use a scrubber if needed.

For persistent dirt leave the soap solution on the floor for 5 minutes and then with a clean cloth remove it again. Rinse your cloth regularly with clean water and then wash the floor for a last time with cleaning soap as first described. Give the floor time to dry.

Your floor is now clean, but will look dull and pretty sad.

Step 2: Applying Much Needed Maintenance

Depending on which finish type your newly discovered floor has - varnish/lacquer or wax/oil - you will need a suitable maintenance product. Power Wax or Wax-polish on a varnished floor will create a slippery surface.

If you are not sure what type of finish is originally used you can try to determine this as follows:

In an inconspicuous area (a corner or behind a door), apply two drops of water. If, within ten minutes white spots appear under the drops of water, the floor has a wax/oil finish. (To remove the white spots, gently rub the spots with 000 steel wool dampened with wax.) If the finish does not flake from scratching with a coin, and white spots do not appear from the drops of water, the floor has a surface (lacquered/varnished) finish.
(If the floor is very old/battered the whole finish layer might have gone and drops of water will turn it very dark, then it is high time to light sand the floor to remove any residue of the old finish and apply a brand new finish)

For a varnished/lacquered floor most maintenance products come in the form of a polish. For an oiled/waxed floor you have the choice between a polish or a hard wax (power wax). If your floor is really dull, and looks rather tired, it's best to apply power wax - it's a bit more hand-and-knee work, but your floor will definitely love you for it.

Polishes: Shake the closed bottle firmly, open the lid and sprinkle the polish undiluted over your floor and use an applicator to spread it out. Leave to dry out for 10 - 15 minutes.

Hard wax (power wax): Scoop some wax out of the tin and drop it on your floor. Spread and rub the wax out with a non-fluffy cloth, over small areas at a time. Leave to dry out for 10 - 15 minutes.

If your old floor looks really tired apply a second coat of the power wax in the same way.

Step 3: Buffing the floor

Buffing your floor after applying the maintenance product will give a better result.

Most electric small buffing machines are too light for this work, and they will hardly have any buffing effect on your wooden floor. Either use a semi-professional buffer with a large white pad, or an 'old-fashioned' style buffing-block made of cast-iron (weights 7 kg, but still works best... and it comes with our 100% guarantee!)

The movement of the pad or buffing block will warm the applied maintenance product, spreading it out more evenly, and allowing the wood to absorb it better. Plus it reduces the time your floor feels slippery. After every buffing stroke you will see your floor come back to life more and more, until you've brought it back to its original, sparkling lustre. An oiled/wax floor especially will start to show its natural beautiful character once again.

It's recommended that you apply a maintenance product at least every 5 - 6 months, and more often in heavy traffic areas. This will keep your wooden floor protected against dirt and drips, and feeds the wood for long term durability.

Congratulations

You are now the proud owner of a valuable, durable, easy to clean and anti-allergic original parquet flooring. Remember, a newly installed parquet floor would have set you back £125.00 - £145.00 per sq m.

With these 3 easy steps you can achieve this labour of love for a lot less! Take good care of it now, it will reward you for years and years to come!

7 Easy Steps to Repair/Restore your Design Parquet Floor

Guide value £8.97
[Extra info available online - www.woodmanual.co.uk]

Hidden Treasures exposed

What is a nicer surprise than to remove the carpet from a room in your home and to discover a valuable original parquet floor is hiding beneath it! Especially when you consider that installing a brand new parquet floor costs around £125.00 - £145.00 per sq m. And that's just for a simple herringbone or basket weave pattern.

Your new discovery will at least need some TLC to bring back its grand luster it had before it was 'covered-up', see our "3 easy steps to clean and maintain your parquet floor" PDF for this. 9 times out of 10 that's all it needs really.

If your floor is missing some blocks, has damaged blocks – damages from plumbing comes to mind - or you notice areas where the blocks no longer stuck firmly down on the underfloor just follow the **7 Easy Steps below** to repair/restore it and start enjoying your valuable, easy to clean and anti-allergic original parquet floor in no time at all. For all materials needed we've included **a list of quality products** underneath.

Step 1: Check for any missing, damaged or loose blocks

Always check the whole floor if blocks are no longer firmly attached to the underfloor – you notice either some movement when walking on it or a hollow sound when you 'knock-on-wood'. Even if your floor is obviously missing blocks – removed for adding central heating or other plumbing/building work – check the rest of the floor too.

Because most original English parquet floors have small tongue and grooves to lock them together you need to handle the removing of loose/damaged blocks with care – you don't want to loosen connecting blocks needlessly. Missing blocks can be sourced perhaps from another room which you do not plan to restore (or try any cupboards in or around the room – you'll be amazed how often a parquet floor was installed in there too!), or from reclamation yards. Before you set out to find replacements note the exact size of the existing blocks, there were plenty different types of wood blocks in Imperial measurements around when these floors were popular (1930 – 1970). Also make sure the reclaimed blocks you find are from the same source to prevent very different wood species or colours ending up in your restored floor.

Step 2: Clean blocks and underfloor

Old parquet floors normally were fixed down with Bitumen – black tar - an 'adhesive' no longer allowed to be used inside the house. Any residue of bitumen has to come off as best as possible. Not the nicest of jobs, but consider it a labour of love. Chiselling, scraping, sanding (will use up loads of paper!), or dipping them in Odourless Kerosene (always be very careful with chemicals, wear gloves and face-protection!) will remove most of it. Placing the blocks in a freezer first will make it easier to chisel or scrape off – the Bitumen becomes very brittle. Make sure any Bitumen is also removed out of all grooves.

The underfloor (concrete or sheet material) must also be cleared of old ridges of Bitumen and if possible thick remaining layers.
Any residue of Bitumen will affect the bonding time of the modern adhesive you use to install the blocks back. Where normally it takes between 6 – 8 hours, the residue could increase this to 14 or even over 72 hours!

(In those cases where a whole floor has to re-installed and the underfloor is covered with a (thick) bitumen layer, read the advice from one of our BwfA colleagues in the preparation section of our book first.)

Step 3: Levelling the underfloor

You might discover your underfloor where blocks have been removed is rather uneven. Or the removing the Bitumen has damaged the concrete or sheet material. You can use acrylic levelling compound to level a concrete floor out as best as possible – 3mm maximum per coat. Always read the instructions carefully before you begin with this type of job! And even though it is non-water based, allow sufficient time for the compound to dry before you start installing the wood blocks back.
For uneven sheet material you can try to level it out with a hand sander or nailing/stapling thin sheets of hardboard onto it – smooth side down!

Step 4: Re- installing blocks

Have a good look at the existing pattern your parquet floor is laid in, you will get the best result when following this as precise as possible.

Take your time, but don't be too afraid when small gaps appear between the blocks. Gaps should be kept as small as possible – hence our advice to clean of the Bitumen from grooves – but will appear nonetheless. Nothing to worry about too much, most of them can be filled after wards, plus original and modern parquet floors will have tiny gaps too due to the seasonal changes in air humidity – making the blocks expand and shrink slightly, a very natural phenomenon.

Us a notched trowel to spread a modern parquet adhesive on the underfloor, this will create ridges of adhesive onto which you firmly place the blocks. For small areas you can use the so-called trowel-knife (only 8cm wide).

The ridges will spread out under the block, giving it an even coverage. Small dips in the floor or block will be covered too this way – not when you spread out the adhesive in just a thin layer. But please remember: **adhesive is not a filler** for deep or large dips in the underfloor (see step 3).

Keep a cloth at hand to wipe of any spillage of the adhesive from the surface of the blocks – once dried it is harder to clean it off.

If needed – especially when you sourced reclaimed blocks – cut the blocks to the right size with a jigsaw and install them into the pattern. It might be necessary to remove the tongue of some blocks but that's not a problem – the modern adhesive you use will keep the blocks in place.

Step 5: Sanding the whole floor

For the best result and a very uniform finish on the whole floor it is best to sand the whole area, not just the re-installed blocks. Remember – the more Bitumen was left on the blocks and/or underfloor the longer it will take for the blocks to bond firmly and the longer you'll have to wait before you can start sanding. You don't want the blocks to start moving around and creating wide gaps!

(If your existing finish layer is in decent state and you managed to source blocks with a similar decent finish you can skip the sanding, filling and applying a new finish steps. Congratulations then on a repaired, valuable and durable floor covering. Read our "Maintenance **tip**" for further information on how to keep your floor healthy, durable and valuable.)

Depending on the old finish layer of the original parquet floor you might have to clean off that layer first before you start sanding – layers of wax will clog-up your sanding paper very fast, making it useless and could spread the wax all over the place! If this is the case you first have to remove the old wax with special Wax Remover or White Spirit – try this out in a corner. Make sure there is enough ventilation in the room when applying any of these products.

Start with vacuum-cleaning the floor.

Use a belt-sander for this part of the job, the endless sanding paper won't leave scatter marks on your wood floor like a drum-sander can (because of the metal rod that has to keep the sheet of sanding paper fixed to the drum). An so-called smaller edge-sander will help you sand edges and the corners of the room where the large sander can't reach. Most professional hire companies will have a combi-offer: belt-sander and edge-sander for a weekend at reduced prices.

If you notice many height differences between the blocks, especially where old meets new – the reclaimed blocks – start with **grit 40**. It's advised to sand with the grain, but herringbones and various other patterns could make this a bit problematic. Nothing to worry about, the various sanding rounds you will have to make will sort this.

Start in one corner of the room and 'walk' the belt-sander across to the other wall, walk back sanding over the same area – with a belt-sander this is possible, a drum-sander might refuse to be walked back. At your starting wall start the next 'row' overlapping the first row half to prevent sharp edges where the sanding machine has done its work. After you've done the last row this way, turn 90 degrees and redo the whole room in the same way.

Place **grit 40** paper on the edge-sander and tackle the areas the belt-sander couldn't reach. Because the movement of the edge-sander is different (circular) than the belt-sander (straight) you could see little circular sanding marks on overlapping areas. Don't try to sand them away with the edge sander – it will only become worse. Following sanding rounds will clear most of them anyway.

Vacuum-clean the whole floor.

Repeat the whole task now with **grit 80**. Before you start sanding, empty the sand-dust collecting bag, you'll need the dust of grit 80 – clean dust – for mixing with the wood-filler later. The dust from the first sanding will contain dirt and residue of the old finish layer. After finishing round 2 vacuum-clean the whole floor.

Step 6: Filling gaps and last sanding round

If you want to fill the gaps in your wood floor mix the collected sand dust from the second sanding round with the special wood-filler. Don't make too much at once, it dries rather quickly. Fill the larger gaps with a scraper as best as possible, don't worry about excess filler on the wood blocks, the third sanding round will remove it. If you want you can also 'plaster' the whole floor with a thin layer of filler, using a flat trowel, to fill almost every tiny gap.

After you're satisfied you've filled all gaps you wanted to fill leave the applied filler to dry out sufficiently, 30 to 60 minutes depending on how deep the gaps were.
Then use sanding paper **grit 120** for the third sanding round, this will remove the excess wood filler and give your wood floor the smoothest surface, ready to have a new finish applied to it. Follow the same pattern with the belt-sander as before and end with the edge-sander.

Or - if you can get one - use a so-called Trio-sander for the last sanding round. It is a still rather new innovation and should only be used when working with a higher grit. Because of the circular movement and speed of the three disks underneath the machine you run the risk of 'being swept away' by the machine when using a rougher grit (like 40 or even 80). Most professional sander hire companies will have one and it will give you an even better result than using a belt-sander for the last sanding round. It will also be able to remove sanding marks from your wood floor, especially on the 'border' of belt-sander and edge-sander (not all, see also our leaflet "What not to expect").

When you use the Trio-sander use **grit 100** instead of 120. The speed of the disks creates a very smooth surface on your wood floor, grit 100 then compares with the same finish grit 120 on the belt and edge sander will give you.

Step 7: Applying new finish

Oils will show off your restored floor best, bringing out its natural character in a none-glossy way. The oil will penetrate the wood for long term protection and the wax will create your wear and tear layer, protecting your floor against dirt and drips. If you prefer a varnished or lacquered finish you'll have to sand again with grit 150 to prepare the wood as best as possible for a varnish/lacquer finish.

Always, always read the instructions of the product you're going to use.
See our chapter: "Which Oil to Use when" also, especially when your original floor has a tropical nature.

Job done!

You could notice some local patches appearing duller or shinier than the rest of the floor. This could mean the wood there has absorbed more or less oil than its neighbouring blocks. Don't apply a third coat of HardWaxOil, but buff the area lightly. If this doesn't seem to help, wait a few days to see if it 'evens-out'. If it still appears differently than the rest of your floor apply some power wax or wax-polish locally to feed it. 9 times out of 10 this will do the trick.
You can place most furniture back in the room once the second coat has dried for 8 hours. **Wait 10 days** before you place rugs on top of your newly restored wood floor, HardWaxOil takes 10 days to cure completely. It will however protect your floor against dirt and drips immediately!

Congratulations

You now have a beautifully restored, valuable and durable floor covering!

Remember, a newly installed parquet floor would have set you back £125.00 - £145.00 per sq m. With these 7 easy steps you do this labour of love for a lot less!

Take good care of it now (wooden floors have the extra benefit of easy-maintenance) and it will continue to reward you for many years to come for all the TLC you've spent on it.

Products and tools recommended and used by Wood You Like Ltd and other professionals

suitable parquet adhesive: Lecol5500, B92 (F.Ball)
various types of notched trowels
HardWaxOil (natural and colours - testers available too)
Euku oil 1 with Leha StepStop
HardWaxOil applicator
and for maintenance see our tips on maintenance

NOTES

Lightning Source UK Ltd.
Milton Keynes UK
31 January 2011

166700UK00004B/6/P